THE FROST OF LOST WORDS: THE HOLY SPIRIT AND THE WRITER

By Stephen Shepherd

Copyright ©2023 by Stephen Shepherd (Higher Ground Books & Media) All rights reserved. No part of this publication may be reproduced in any form, stored in a retrieval system, or transmitted in any form, or by any means (electronic, mechanical, photocopying, recording or otherwise) without prior permission by the copyright owner and the publisher of this book.

Scripture taken from King James Bible, Copyright 1990, by Thomas Nelson, Inc. All rights reserved worldwide.

Higher Ground Books & Media
P.O. Box 2914
Springfield, OH 45501-2914
www.highergroundbooksandmedia.com
1-937-970-0554

Because of the dynamic nature of the Internet, any web addresses or links contained in this book may have changed since publication and may no longer be valid. The views expressed in the work are solely those of the author and do not necessarily reflect the views of the publisher, and the publisher hereby disclaims any responsibility for them.

Any people depicted in stock imagery are being used for illustrative purposes only.

ISBN (Paperback): 978-1-955368-31-5

Printed in the United States of America 2023

THE FROST OF LOST WORDS: THE HOLY SPIRIT AND THE WRITER

By Stephen Shepherd

CONTENTS

Chapter 1 The Holy Spirit and the Writing Process
Essay 1 The Supernatural Force of Inspiration
Essay 2 The Holy Spirit and the Writer's Space
Essay 3 Autobiographical Writing and the Holy Spirit
Essay 4 The Holy Spirit Knows You as a Writer
Essay 5 The Writing Stage and the Holy Spirit
Essay 6 Patience is Supplied by the Holy Spirit
Essay 7 Rough Draft, Writing Styles, and the Holy Spirit
Essay 8 The Holy Spirit Elevates Meaning
Essay 9 The Holy Spirit's Guidance
Essay 10 The Holy Spirit Develops the Rough Draft
Essay 11 The Holy Spirit in the Revision Stage
Chapter 2 Writer's Need the Holy Spirit's Protection
Essay 12 Satan Endorses a Destructive Lifestyle
Essay 13 Satan's Intrusions on a Writer
Essay 14 Satan's Economic Influence on Writers
Essay 15 Satan's Use of Fear on a Writer
Chapter 3 Connecting with the Holy Spirit
Essay 16 Understanding the Holy Spirit
Essay 17 A Writer's Spiritual Identity
Essay 18 Using Satan's World for Moral Instruction
Essay 19 Writing the Unbiased Truth
Essay 20 Writing to Draw Closer to God
Essay 21 The Hidden Spirit of the Writer
Essay 22 Make Holiness Your Focus
Essay 23 Greed and Literary Success
Chapter 4 Some Literary Works Influenced by the Holy Spirit
Essay 24 John Cheever: The Enormous Radio
Essay 25 Kurt Vonnegut: Breakfast of Champions
Essay 26 Joseph Heller: Catch 22
Essay 27 TS Eliot: The Love Song of J Alfred Prufrock
Essay 28 Conclusion: Connotation, Denotation, and the Holy Spirit

The Frost of Lost Words

PREFACE

I don't pretend to be a Bible scholar. I am simply a devoted practitioner of writing who over the past 50 years of writing has experienced some common threads of writing's purpose. To me, writing is a two-way street. The writer gives something of themselves to their writing, and writing gives something back to them. What a writer receives in return from practicing the art and craft of writing may, in fact, be more important than what they give to the reader. You see, writing can be much more than a one-way secular experience of disseminating information. In fact, writing can be a spiritual journey, if you let it become one. This book is exacted towards this end by making writing a sacred practice that can bring you closer to Jesus by understanding His presence through the Holy Spirit while you write. In doing so, I can only relate to you what I have experienced. To this end, I write in the Holy Spirit's presence. How else can I explain writing for years without conscious effort while trying to keep up with my own pen? Like everything in life, writing is a gift given by God to people He has chosen to do His will on earth. Therefore, people are called by God to be writers. As such, He nurtures the writer through the Holy Spirit as provided by Jesus. God does not appoint people a vocation like writing and then abandoned them to their own devices. No, God not only creates aspiring writers, but He also guides and encourages them to become better writers through the supernatural urgings of the Holy Spirit. Thus, The Holy Spirit guides the writer through all phases of writing from finding a topic to pressing into place the final period of the last sentence. From my experience, writing is a supernatural experience designed by God from start to finish. Consequently, by becoming a better writer, you can also become a better person and one closer to God, if you let Jesus through the Holy Spirit participate. In this book, I have underlined every word when the Holy Spirit helps the writer during the writing process. In turn, these underlined words may help you to discern the Holy Spirit at work in your own writing.

CHAPTER 1 THE HOLY SPIRIT AND THE WRITING PROCESS

Essay 1 The Supernatural Force of Inspiration

Trying to understand why a writer wrote something is a difficult task because a writer has many motivations. However, behind all those rational motivations for writing there lies a bigger spiritual inspiration for the writer to have written anything at all. What prompted their motivation to write? What compelled the writer by the subject's importance to write about it? For, if we don't examine the larger question of what's behind these motivations, then the true meaning of those written words will be lost. I believe that before the writer thinks of a topic and even begins to write the first word, there is a supernatural force being exerted on why a writer chooses a topic. "Ye have not chosen me, but I have chosen you, and ordained you, that ye should go and bring forth fruit" (John 15:16). From the billions of possible topics in the world, a writer chooses to write about only one of them. So why did the author choose one topic while rejecting all others? The answer to that question is found in the supernatural promptings of the Holy Spirit. In short, the writer doesn't decide which topic to write about; God does. "But when they shall lead you and deliver you up, take no thought beforehand what ye shall speak, neither do ye premeditate: but whatsoever shall be given you in that hour that speak ye, for it is not ye that speak, but the Holy Ghost" (Mark 13:11). So, in my opinion, writing is a supernatural act from the first inspiration to the last letter; Jesus prompts us about what to write and how to write it because the Holy Spirit intercedes on a writer's behalf and provides direction. We, as writers, don't choose how we write, what we write, or for whom we write it! God does. Wolfgang

Amadeus Mozart in a letter once described his manner of composing. "When and how my ideas come, I know not; nor can I force them." He further stated that he could see the entire musical composition in his mind as a finished piece before he wrote like a fine picture or a beautiful statue. In short, Mozart could see a completed composition with all the instruments playing before he wrote it (Gardner 358-360). Therefore, what prompted Mozart to see in his mind's eye an entire finished musical composition and to hear all the musical instruments playing simultaneously? I submit that it was supernatural energy provided by the Holy Spirit!

In the Old Testament, God gives Moses' instructions about how to build His temple. The instructions are so explicit that God includes who will be the workmen to complete the project. God has given each workman particular talents to complete the Tabernacle. In the Old Testament some workers are called out by name and the talents that God has given to each of them. The Lord said to Moses, "See I have called by name Bezalel the son of Uri, son of Hur, of the tribe of Judah, and I have filled him with the Spirit of God, with ability and intelligence, with knowledge and all craftsmanship, to devise [create] artistic designs, to work in gold and silver, and bronze, in cutting stones for setting, and in carving wood, to work in every craft..." (Exodus 35:30-35). Each worker was given special talents by God. In this way, God knew that His Temple would be completed in exactly the way He wanted it constructed. Whether God gave these workmen their natural talent since birth or whether they just woke up one morning with it, no one knows.

Because God controls everything, why would He not control the writer's inspiration and impulse to write? It is God's <u>inspiration</u> on a person through the Holy Spirit that allows the writer to have an imaginative and creative mind. In fact, without the Holy Spirit's involvement in the writing process, no thoughts could ever be created, much less written. "Every good gift and every perfect gift is from above, and cometh down from the Father of lights, with whom is no variableness, neither shadow of turning" (James 1:17). Most writers who have practiced the writing craft for a while have experienced at some point a supernatural force hijacking their minds, pens, and keyboards. This supernatural experience is called by writers as being in the "writing zone" or simply "in the zone." Writers feel like they're in a "writing zone" when their thoughts turn to words on the page so easily and naturally that it feels like the words are coming from some other place beyond themselves; it is like the writer is no longer writing the words but following along like in dictation. Sometimes the thoughts and words flow so fast that some writers feel like they are racing to keep pace with their own work. Of course, all writers will take credit for having written the words while in "the zone" because it is usually some of their best writing. But did they really write it? I submit that the power of warp speed thoughts turning into war speed words written on warp speed pages is coming from The Holy Spirit. In fact, while a fiction writer is working in a "writing zone," many times they do not even know the direction of their own story. Without knowing where a story writing is going, they just keep writing blindly forward in the dark, moving ahead as quickly as possible in the development of characters and action. For example, John Cheever was in "the writing zone" when he finished his novel *The Falconer*. Upon completing the novel's last word, Cheever jumped up from his chair and ran to his wife to announce the main character's fate because he did not know it himself. He was very pleased with his novel's ending, but he was as surprised as any reader about its outcome. It sounds like Cheever had "other worldly" supernatural involvement. "But you will receive power when the Holy Spirit has come upon you..." (Acts 1:8).

    Being in "the writing zone" and receiving the words from beyond yourself from the Holy Spirit is not a new concept. In fact, there are many theories about how the writers of the scripture interacted with the Holy Spirit. Certainly, I'm not a Bible scholar, but all the following theories espouse the Holy Spirit's involvement in the writing of scripture. Philo of Alexandria (20 BCE to 40 CE) in *De Vita Moysis* "proposed what was termed the Automatic Writing Theory regarding the inspiration for the writing of the scriptures, in which the human author becomes possessed by God and loses consciousness of self, surrendering to the divine spirit and its communicatory powers" (iii, no.23). Then, the Negative Assistance Theory by Jacque Bonfrievre (1573-1642) suggested that the intervention of the Holy Spirit into the writer's consciousness to write the Bible occurred only as needed, in order to prevent them from making mistakes (Metzger). Other alternate names for the Negative Assistance Theory include Concept of Inspiration, Theory of Inspiration, and Partial Inspiration (Swayer). Then, the Positive Assistance Theory asserts that the Holy Spirit and the writer collaborated to write the Bible by empowering the writer to communicate what God wanted. The Verbal Dictation Theory states that God dictated the words of the Bible to the writer. The Dynamic Inspiration Theory suggests that the thoughts contained in the Bible are inspired, but the words were left to the individual writers (Lea). You get the idea. The Holy Spirit's impact on the writing of Holy Scripture is unquestionable. Of course, all these theories, as well as many others, were written about how much – and not whether -- the Holy Spirit was involved in the writing of the Bible. While some scholars might dismiss one theory in favor of another, most scholars will agree that at some level the Holy Spirit's supernatural intervention did occur, and – in my opinion -- it still occurs today when many writers experience being gifted words from somewhere else beyond themselves while being in "the writing zone." When God is at work in the world, why wouldn't He help a writer compose? In my opinion, He does. Through the Holy Spirit's promptings as provided by Jesus, God works His purpose on earth through writers today.

Although I believe that the supernatural intervention of the Holy Spirit in writing does happen today, writers must have faith and pray during the writing process that the Holy Spirit will supernaturally <u>guide</u> them. Right now, as I write this book, there isn't an outline – no blueprint for writing. I'm writing from a total dependence on the Holy Spirit for each word. Sometimes, I get terrified that my words will end in mid-sentence because I'm so reliant on the Holy Spirit for them. Some days, I can't write, and I know it because the Holy Spirit tells me to take a break. And, if I defy the Holy Spirit's <u>advice</u> about taking a break and rely on my own judgement, then the writing is not much fun nor any good. However, with the Spirit <u>guiding</u> me the words flow like clean mountain air. Therefore, a writer's awareness about the Holy Spirit's involvement in their work and the <u>directive role</u> the Spirit plays in the writing process is extremely important. For instance, Writer's Block occurs when a writer refuses to pray for the Holy Spirit's <u>involvement</u> in their work. The Holy Spirit can be both a comforting and supernatural guiding force for writers who tend to rely on themselves too much. In short, writers afflicted by writer's block are trying too hard to do everything by themselves, and they try so hard that it paralyzes their thoughts. Furthermore, Writer's Block does not have a life expectancy; it can afflict a writer for months and years, and only by praying to God, Jesus, and the Holy Spirit (The Holy Trinity) will it end. In fact, Satan has used writer's block to end many promising writing careers; it is one of Satan's oldest tools used against writers.

Questions

1. Have you ever written in the writing zone?
2. If so, what did it feel like?
3. When the writing zone ended, could you remember what you had written?

4. If not, why not?

Essay 2   The Holy Spirit and a Writer's Space

A writer always needs a sense of dedicated space where good writing can take place. The place where good writing can take place varies by individual, but the goal is the same: to find a place that consistently motivates a writer toward good writing. Inexperienced writers like to think that they can write anywhere, and this is true to some extent; writing can, indeed, take place anywhere. However, good writing demands an environment conducive to success. A good and consistent place where good writing occurs is like having the reassuring comfort of a soft pillow or a warm blanket, and the Holy Spirit provides a writer with this sense of <u>security and hope</u>. If God can guide the Israelites out of Egypt into the Promise Land, He can certainly guide your writing. This is what God says about guiding the Israelites, "And I come down to deliver them out of the hand of the Egyptians, and to bring them up out of that land unto a good land and a large, unto a land flowing with milk and honey…" (Exodus 3:8) I believe that all writers are on a similar spiritual journey and a leap of faith in God is necessary to withstand the world's harsh realities to find the promise land of words. This may be an excessive comparison, but these words do come from somewhere else and are not easily accessed because they are given to a writer by the supernatural power of God. To gain access to the energy of these supernatural words, a writer needs to pray to believe in the comfort of the Holy Spirit's presence. Feeling the comfort of the Holy Spirit while in your favorite writing place won't guarantee that you will always write better, but it will increase the odds that you will.

Some inexperienced writers dismiss praying to Jesus and the Holy Spirit in a comfortable writing space as mere superstition. However, praying to Jesus through the Holy Spirit for advice to secure a higher level of physical, emotional, and physical contentment makes sense because an increase in comfort often transfers to an increase in the quality of your work. In short, becoming <u>enlightened</u> by the Holy Spirit about your needs as a writer also produces a corresponding emotional response that's conducive to better work. I know writers who need loud music in the background to write, while other writers need total silence. Some writers eat Cheetos while they write, while other writers don't allow food and drink within twenty feet of their desk. Over time, the Holy Spirit resolves the issues related to what constitutes a good writing space by <u>guiding</u> the writer to accept or reject certain writing needs. For example, as a beginning writer, you probably weren't consciously looking for a good place to write, but over time you found yourself by the Holy Spirit's promptings returning to the same place again and again because of its <u>comfort</u> and familiarity. In short, the space felt right, and it helped you to concentrate on your writing. This comfortable feeling derived from being in a certain writing place was given to you by the Holy Spirit. Virginia Woolf wrote in a storage room in the basement while sitting in an old comfortable armchair. Agatha Christie wrote most of her mystery novels while eating apples and taking a bath in an old Victorian bathtub. Edith Wharton wrote while covered up with blankets in bed with her dog by her side. Stephen King wrote his first novel *Carrie* at a make-shift desk sandwiched between a washer and dryer in the laundry room. Because the Holy Spirit <u>prompted</u> them to use that space for writing during certain times of the day, when they went to that <u>comfortable</u> space, they had already mentally committed themselves to the act of writing. Stephen King said, "I try to get six pages a day. I start in the morning between 8 and 8:30 am." Hemingway wrote *For Whom The Bell Tolls*, *The Snows of Kilimanjaro*, and other literary classics in a small second-story writing room overlooking his swimming pool at 907 Whitehead St., Key West, Florida. He also had a favorite time to write – at sunrise and early in the morning. This act of repetitive involvement as performance ritual increases a writer's confidence that good writing will take place. It is much like settling in with Jesus in your heart through constant prayer. Prayer is also a repetitive practice that elicits a form of comfort. Instead of a physical place where the Holy Spirit has taken you to take <u>comfort</u> from the world to write, with prayer you gain spiritual comfort from the world within the protective walls of God. Jesus stated, "But the Comforter, which is the Holy Ghost, whom the Father will send in my name, he shall teach you all things, and bring all things to your remembrance, whatsoever I have said unto you" (John 14:26).

    Therefore, attempting to write while in the Holy Spirit's choice of a place is a very promising start. Because it was prompted by the Holy Spirit, this comfortable place has a sacredness about it because the Holy Spirit is embracing you while you are there. It's a supernatural place where through prayer the energy of the Holy Spirit can be released and can improve your life and improve your writing. Just like the Holy Spirit had you pursue the power of a quiet place in the physical world to write, the Holy Spirit also provides you with the supernatural power of God to actually do the writing. When the Holy Spirit's presence anoints your writing while you're in "the writing zone," your thoughts produce more meaningful words. Only God can direct a writer's path to <u>creative thought</u> and only He can infuse the <u>joy</u> that you get from following the supernatural flow of it. As mentioned previously, some writers call being in the Holy Spirit's presence as being in *the writing zone* because the ease of their writing thoughts and skills suddenly improves. In short, the Holy Spirit makes it possible for them to live up to the supernatural challenge to create. When the content of a writer's skills lives up to their supernatural calling, then the Holy Spirit releases a sense of <u>joy</u> in the writer with that accomplishment. However, without the Holy Spirit's <u>comfort</u>, <u>guidance</u>, and <u>involvement</u>, the act of writing is less joyful and more tedious because it is reduced to the physical act of touching a keyboard or holding a pen. Therefore, the mind might be able to transfer a word to a page, but only the Holy Spirit can bring <u>joy</u> and <u>passion</u> to the creative moment.

In a way, writing with or without the Holy Spirit is like the physical act of petting a dog on the head. You can just physically pet the dog on the head, as in just performing a physical act. Or you can feel the comfort that you're giving to the dog while petting it, as well as the comfort being derived by you from petting the dog. Although the same physical act of petting the dog is being performed, the depth of experience of it differs in how it transacts the information. In the first instance, where just the physical act of petting the dog is done, the participant derives very little pleasure from the experience because the action is rote and superficial and because it does not transact the emotion from you to the dog or from the dog to you. However, in the second instance, where the person is cognizant and senses the emotional involvement of both living things in the petting transaction, then the act of petting the dog is elevated from the mere physical act into a heartfelt spiritual connection. Now, two living things are communicating and making a connection about the value found in their lives by their association, and they both enjoy being alive and being in the company of one another. Therefore, the axiom that "A dog is man's best friend" is accurate because it is about creating a spiritual bond between two living things. When this happens, man and dog truly are best friends. However, when that spiritual bond is not accessed, then behavior with potential Holy Spirit participation is abandoned in favor of just the bare physical act. Of course, Satan encourages moving on the earth to just the physical actions in life because it emotionally disconnects people from other people and people from other living things. In the end, it breeds resentment and distrust. In short, when a man can't trust his dog, and his dog can't trust the man, then all that remains is the physical shallowness of a pet on the head and mistrust ensues on both sides. Thus, when writers can't recognize the spiritual qualities found in every human action in life then they lose the heightened angle of vision where the spiritual energy of God is found for their writing; thus, they cannot transfer it to their life or to their work. The involvement of the Holy Spirit heightens a writer's awareness about the sacredness of all life and this increased spiritual awareness makes both their life and their writing better and more meaningful.

In fact, nothing truly creative can be accomplished without the involvement of the Holy Spirit because it provides the joy from an innovative act that comes from the heart. Therefore, you may be able to physically outline and write a mystery novel with the reasoning provided by an educated mind, but the pure joy and essence of yourself that makes your mystery novel unique from other writers is supplied by the Holy Spirit's inspiration. I have read hundreds of novels that read like another author's writing. The difference between the inspirational first novel and the imitative second novel is that the initial first story had the creative force of the Holy Spirit behind it, which made that story different, creative, and wholly individual and original. So, the Holy Spirit's creative power is within all writers to help them to live and to write better and more creatively, but they must pray for Jesus and the Holy Spirit's involvement in their lives and writing, and they must read the Bible to access the Holy Spirit's supernatural power of guidance. Without the Holy Spirit's power, writing is often unimaginative, imitative, and uninspiring because the Holy Spirit's creative spirit and the joy released while creating it have remained untapped. Therefore, many writers do what they can physically to write by using the same writing space to improve their work, but they often neglect to find their ultimate creative self by praying for the inspirational power of their Holy

Spirit. "God is a Spirit: and they that worship him must worship him in the spirit and in truth" (John 4:24).

Therefore, writers need to do all that they can both physically by finding a comfortable writing space and spiritually by wholeheartedly praying to God, Jesus, and the Holy Spirit for help when they write. Each time that any writer senses and follows the Holy Spirit's <u>advice</u> to improve their life, their writing also improves because the quality of their spiritual relationship with the Holy Trinity has improved, and this supernatural power migrates into the quality of their writing life. However, sometimes experiencing the Holy Spirit's presence can be very brief, like seeing a flash of color or a glint of light. Virginia Woolf saw a glint of light one morning coming through a window in her house and the Holy Spirit's involvement inspired her to write the novel *To the Lighthouse*. Therefore, the act of writing can be much more than just a physical exercise; it can also be a spiritual experience; that is, if a writer lets it become one.

In John 3:5, "Jesus answered, Verily, verily, I say unto thee, Except a man be born of water and of the Spirit, he cannot enter into the kingdom of God. That which is born of the flesh is flesh; and that which is which is born of the Spirit is spirit." So, it appears that there is, indeed, a distinction made between things that are derived from the flesh and things that are derived from the Spirit. This distinction is apparent when examining the writing produced in the physical act of writing and the Spiritual quality of the writing produced after the Holy Spirit's involvement. One word written with the physical mind during the writing process is not the same word written in the Spirit during the writing process. The Spirit's involvement in writing adds a noticeably transcendent quality to each word and elevates it to a higher place above a physical word. In short, a physical word might communicate a thought; but it does not convey the passion of the writing moment. This happens only with the Holy Spirit's involvement by providing the writer with spiritual inspiration to find just the "right" word. And only when the Holy Spirit is present in the writing process will a writer be satisfied with their work. "Howbeit when he, the Spirit of truth, is come, he will guide you in all truth… (John 16:13). That's why some writers are never satisfied with their writing and that's why a writer can write a first good novel but then write a not-so-good second novel. The Holy Spirit was at work advising the writer in the first novel and not so much in the second novel.

Writer Virginia Woolf experienced the difference between the Holy Spirit being involved in her writing and in the subsequent success of it. Woolf planned, wrote, and revised her writing using the same physical process, but she found that the physical process of writing often did not yield the same quality of work. "I write two pages of arrant nonsense, after straining; I write variations of every sentence; compromises; bad shots; possibilities; till my writing book is like a lunatic's dream. Then I trust inspiration on re-reading; and pencil them into some sense. Still, I am not satisfied" (Woolf). Thus, the physical process of prewriting, writing, and rewriting can be repeated without similar successful results. This implies that some other influence is being exerted on the writing process to elicit better writing, and I submit that that influence is the power of the Holy Spirit. A reader knows when the Holy Spirit has connected a word to a writer's brain. The word's novelty and creative nuance leaps off the page. This power of the imagination and the resulting emotional charge cannot be found in a mere physical word. If a writer accepts the Holy Spirit into their work, the difference in how the Holy Spirit's involvement impacts the writer's work becomes evident, especially when a writer searches for just the "right" word. The vision in a writer's mind of seeing just the right word to write comes from the Holy Spirit, and this vision of being able to see the right word to improve writing will not reach a nonbeliever's brain. The truth relayed and displayed from just the right word can only come from God. While a functional physical word will suffice in most secular circumstances, it will not suffice in a spiritually infused circumstance because the addition of the Holy Spirit's power elevates the words found and used. In short, writing can be a transcendent and sacred experience -- if you let it!

John 3:8 illustrates how dependent the writer is on the Holy Spirit for finding the correct word. As mentioned previously, writing is really an act of faith that you will be able to produce at least one word on the page. The leap of faith that it takes to become a writer takes courage. What if I don't have anything important to write? What if I find out my life is so boring that I can't be a writer? And other personal questions surface. To produce any kind of creative work from nothing is unsettling because every artist must rely on something (i.e., The Holy Spirit) beyond their physical self to prompt <u>creativity</u>, <u>inspiration,</u> and <u>direction</u>. Even experienced writers like Virginia Woolf knew the terror of facing a blank page; in this terror, a writer must flee from their physical self to find comfort in their Spiritual self where the first word lives. It is in this unknown and unclear vision from no word on the page to one word on the page and the anxiety attached to it that the writer fears most. John 3:8 addresses the uneasiness of this transitory stage of life and writing when the writer needs the relief of the Holy Spirit from *the frost of lost words* and from the known demons of a blank page. "The wind bloweth where it listeth, and thou hearest the sound thereof, but canst not tell whence it cometh, and whither it goeth: so is every one that is born of the Spirit."

Questions

1. Do you have a favorite place to write?
2. If so, how does it make you feel?
3. Do you think your writing improves while there?
4. Can you explain why it is comfortable?
5. What or who enables you to write better while there?

Essay 3 Autobiographical Writing and The Holy Spirit

The writing process moves normally through three stages: prewriting, writing, and rewriting. In the prewriting process, all the planning that should go into a piece of writing occurs. In the prewriting stage, the writer takes a risk by brainstorming for a topic. But this doesn't guarantee that all a writer's prewriting thoughts will work out as planned. When you begin to write some other supernatural force –the Holy Spirit -- sometimes takes over and some of the intentions of the pre-planning writing stage are often altered by the creative self. Likewise, all the plans for your life won't work out either because both your writing and your life are controlled by God. Then, by praying to God, Jesus, and the Holy Spirit (The Holy Trinity), writers can find strength to discover God's writing plan for them. "As each has received a gift, use it to serve one another, as good stewards of God's varied graces… (1 Peter 4:10-11). Without this vision from the Holy Spirit about what to do with a God-given writing talent, a writer can wander around aimlessly looking for direction in the pointless writing forest of life. However, with the Holy Spirit empowerment, the writer can do God's calling and follow His directions. **"We have received not the spirit of the world, but the Spirit which is from God, that we might understand the gifts bestowed on us by God and we impart this in words not taught by human wisdom but taught by the Spirit" (1 Corinthians 2:12 -13).** What a writer was empowered by God to do they can accomplish only if the Holy Spirit is involved.

All writing -- to some degree -- is autobiographical. It's the author's life experience commenting on some aspect of the world. The level of autobiographical material depends on the writing genre. For example, a memoir – if truthful – is totally autobiographical, whereas a science fiction novel might be inspired by some life experience but is mostly a creative transfer by the Holy Spirit of that information. The Holy Spirit's transfer of real-life experience into a fictional experience may contain only a nugget of autobiographical truth, but that one nugget of information was retained in a writer's memory by the Holy Spirit, and it became the catalyst for the writer to move their writing into that fictional direction. For example, the fictional characters found in a novel often intersect with a writer's life. The description and movements of the characters in a novel are promptings from the Holy Spirit's influence on the writer about what is autobiographically important. No writer chooses to write about unimportant things; they choose to write about important things and why it's important to them. Therefore, the Holy Spirit helps the writer to <u>discern</u> what's important to them by the actions of the characters that they create. "I wish that all were as myself am. But each has his own gift from God, one of one kind and one of another" (1 Corinthians 7:7). The description and actions of fictional characters are often based on composite personality traits from many people in a writer's life. It's like a painter mixing colors on a palette, blending just enough of each color to create a dominate impression. Thus, writers' observations in the real world provided by the Holy Spirit enable them to "piece together" many personalities and descriptive traits into one character portrait. Therefore, many descriptions and actions of fictional characters are really a combination of a writer's autobiographical pieces taken from life. For example, I once knew a writer who had written and published a short story in a major magazine where he had combined the personality traits of two of his sisters. When the story was published in a popular magazine, both sisters read it and recognized themselves in the unflattering description of a fictional character, and the writer's sisters wouldn't speak to him for a long time.

    Another writer friend finds all his background information for his fictional characters in the obituary columns of numerous newspapers. He claimed that all the autobiographical information about a character could be found there. In this case, fiction imitates life, and life imitates fiction. So, fiction's distance from a writer's life is very close because it is defined and refined from a writer's autobiographical roots. Yet, what writers choose to remember about their life as autobiographical experience is controlled by the <u>inspiration</u> of the Holy Spirit. "The Spirit of the Lord shall rest upon him, the Spirit of wisdom and understanding, the Spirit of counsel and might, the Spirit of Knowledge and of the fear of the Lord" (Isaiah 11:2). Therefore, The Holy Spirit <u>rewards</u> those writers who can recall the Spirit's <u>promptings</u> and why? Many writers observe, think, and plan for months and years before they begin to write because they are waiting for the inspiration of the Holy Spirit to guide them. For example, Mozart thought about his music for long periods of time. He would hum variations of a musical composition to himself and contemplate where the instruments would be introduced before committing his thoughts to writing. Hence, the Holy Spirit <u>directs</u> a writer even in the planning stages of writing by parsing the writer's total life experience into smaller and more memorable events to be converted into musical notes, fictional characters, scenes, and plots. In short, the Holy Spirit's <u>creative</u> inspiration to a writer is invaluable.

    Subsequently, the Holy Spirit gives the writer <u>insight</u> into their own life and their writing's connection to it. In short, the Holy Spirit inspires writers by giving them vivid memories that remain with them from their own life's importance to be used in their own work. To a writer who does not understand the Holy Spirit's involvement in their life and in their writing, the memories that cling to a writer throughout life may appear to be random, but these thoughts are not random; they are the <u>promptings</u> of the Holy Spirit to bring <u>revelation</u> to the writer's work. Mozart's first biographer stated "His [Mozart's] imagination presented the whole work, when it came to him, clearly and vividly…free and independent of all concerns his spirit could soar in daring flight to the highest regions of art" (Niemetsckek 54-55). Therefore, the Holy Spirit inspires individual remembrances in the writer's mind for the purpose of the writer to use for God. From all other of life's experiences, the writer remembers only a particular event as <u>revealed</u> by the Holy Spirit. "But God hath revealed them unto us by his Spirit: for the Spirit searcheth all things, yea, the deep things of God" (1 Corinthians 2:10).

Thus, while many events in a writer's life cannot be recalled, certain ones can be recalled vividly because of the Holy Spirit's revealing their importance to a writer. Throughout life, the Holy Spirit gives <u>rebirth</u> to experience as recollection to the events of a writer's past to be included in future writings. By the Holy Spirit's inclusion of only certain events, the writer is led by the Spirit to do God's work. In short, the Holy Spirit supplies the supernatural power to the writer's memory <u>to produce the fruit</u> of remembrance to guide the writer's work. "Wherefore by their fruits ye shall know them" (Matthew 7:20). Therefore, the Holy Spirit sorts through the writer's life to make suggestions to the writer about an event's importance. For instance, of all the birthdays that you've had, you can only remember a few; namely, those birthdays that were significant. These remembered birthdays are supplied by the Holy Spirit to a writer to give them moral guidance and comfort in their work. The remembered birthday party can be either a good or bad, but its uniqueness has forged a life-long memory. A writer recalls one birthday because of the <u>intercession</u> of the Holy Spirit, and a writer includes it into the content of their writing because of the Holy Spirit's <u>advice</u>. Whether a writer can recall a memorable experience usually depends on a moral lesson that's learned. The Holy Spirit <u>leads and directs</u> a writer by directing a writer's heart into moral action. "And he that searcheth the hearts knoweth what is the mind of the Spirit, because he maketh intercession for the saints according to the will of God" (Romans 8:27). For a writer the Holy Spirit provides a <u>renewal</u> of important life events in their mind that become the impetus for writing. In turn, the writer recreates these autobiographical events by writing about them in a moral lesson for a reader. Therefore, God reaches the reader with a moral message through the Holy Spirit's influence on the writer.

In James Thurber's short story "The Greatest Man In The World," Thurber introduces the moral concept of humility and how not being humble can kill you. The protagonist Jackie "Pal" Smurch is the first person in aviation history to fly nonstop around the world. Unfortunately, the media and Washington, DC politicos soon discover that Jackie's personality, appearance, and background are very unfit for a national hero or role model. It's true that Jackie Smurch did accomplish a heroic feat, but as a human being Jackie lacked all the personal characteristics of a heroic figure. In fact, his own mother hated her son. When asked by a reporter about the peril involved in her son's around-the-world flight, she carped, "Ah, the hell with him. I hope he drowns." His brother "a weak-minded lad" is currently on the lamb from the law and wanted in several states for the theft of US Post Office money orders, and his father is in jail "somewhere" because he's been in so many jails so often that it's hard to keep track of him. In addition, some of Jackie's own unsavory exploits included once knifing the principal of his high school and stealing an alter cloth from the church after bashing the sacristan in the head with a pot of Easter Lilies.

So, after flying nonstop around the world, Jackie Smurch coasts his rickety bi-plane with its huge axillary gas tanks into a perfect three-point landing at Roosevelt Field, and thousands of people mobbed the airport to get a glimpse of him. Fortunately, Jackie promptly fainted from malnourishment and had to be carried from the plane. His provisions for the non-stop flight around the world included six pounds of salami and 1 gallon of bootleg gin. After he landed his airplane, the media and politicians spirited Jackie away to a remote hospital for 10 days in hopes of instructing him on how to act like a hero. But Jackie wasn't listening to their advice and indignantly replied, "I did it, see? I did it, and I'm talking about it [and] ...When do I start cuttin' in [on the money]." So, Jackie's motivation for attempting his around-the-world flight was to get rich. Of course, former heroic aviators weren't in it for the money or for the glory; they were in it for the patriotism and the challenge, but for Jackie it was all about the money and fame, and it alarmed the press core and Washington elites so much that they arranged one last secret meeting with Jackie to instruct him on how to act humbly like a hero. At this meeting when the US President entered the room, everyone in the room stood up according to protocol, except Jackie, who remained seated in a chair leaned against the back wall where he was busy cleaning his fingernails with a jackknife. When it became apparent to those dignitaries at the meeting that Jackie lacked any assemblance of humility and refused to change his behavior, the President of the United States nodded slightly to a former football player from Rutgers, who tossed Jackie out a ninth story window to his death (Thurber). <u>Humility</u> is given to us by the Holy Spirit, and Thurber's story is about the difference between being a hero and humbly behaving and living like one. In short, the story's theme is an important moral lesson for us all concerning our accomplishments because every physical action without a corresponding spiritual connection is morally dead.

Because the Holy Spirit is co-writing everything a writer writes, good writers know that they are not writing alone. The fact that the Holy Spirit is a <u>co-writer</u> should be a humbling experience for any writer. While writers are taking all the photo opts and kudos, the Holy Spirit is working quietly behind the scenes to help them to succeed. Also, if writers pray to Jesus and thank Him for the assistance of the Holy Spirit, then they are really giving credit where credit is due – to God! Of course, humility among writers is often in short supply. In fact, many writers often compete with other writers as if writing were a track and field event. This false assumption, of course, is more about a writer's ego than about writing improvement. John Cheever once said that "writing is not a competitive sport." And he was right, yet the lack of humility among writers is infamous and easily recognized at social gatherings when the "who is the biggest elephant in the room" competition begins. Writers who lack humility also lack the insight into why God made them a writer. "For whosoever exalteth himself shall be abased; and he that humbleth himself shall be exalted" (Luke 14:11). Overall, suffice it to say that the Holy Spirit did not get involved in your writing so that you could take all the credit. The Holy Spirit got involved in your writing so that you could humbly place the credit for your work at God's feet.

Questions

1. For a writer, why shouldn't memorable events be random?
2. Who prompted you to remember these events?
3. Why did these events remain with you for a lifetime?
4. How are these events connected to writing?

Essay 4 The Holy Spirit Knows You as a Writer

The first rule of writing is to write about what you know. Therefore, for every writer the creative experience is different because their total life experience is different. While one writer might find a writing topic suitable, another writer may not because of the difference in life experience. Therefore, one writer's system to elicit good writing might not work for another writer because they are living in two different personal backgrounds. Their frame of reference for life is different. While writers are often known for gleaning literary techniques from other writers to use in their own work, many times writers are still at a loss to help other writers when it comes to using life as a personal reference point for finding a topic for their writing because one life-sized experience does not fit all. This is because it isn't the physical nature of the life's experience that influences a writer to choose a topic; it is the spiritual meaning in the life's experience through the Holy Spirit that is important to a writer. For example, even the message written by Pontius Pilot on Jesus' crucifixion cross is evidence of God's influence because knowingly or unknowingly Pilot commented on the spiritual significance of the event by his inscription. "And Pilate wrote a title, and put it on the cross. And the writing was 'Jesus of Nazareth the king of the Jews'... and it was written in Hebrew, and Greek, and Latin. Then said the chief priests of the Jews to Pilate, Write not, The King of the Jews; but that he said, I am King of the Jews. Pilate answered, What I have written, I have written" (John 19:19-22). Therefore, during the most significant event in human history, when the Son of God dies for our sins, even Pontius Pilot, a secular Roman Governor, was <u>instructed</u> by God when he wrote the inscription on Jesus' cross in the three most popular languages of the time (i.e., Hebrew, Greek, and Latin). Only God can bind holiness to a piece of writing. Physical revisions may abound, but only through God can the words take on supernatural power. In this case, the hand of God directed Pilot's words to imply that Jesus was innocent and the Son of God.

In addition, the Holy Spirit's involvement gives writers a greater sense of control over their work because they write from the Holy Spirit's guidance. In particular, the Holy Spirit helps the writer in their weakness. For example, most writers don't think about imaginative metaphors until they write them. Then, at that moment when they need one, they are delighted to find one. Many writers believe that they find figurative language like metaphors and similes by accident because they don't plan to write these metaphors and similes in the first place; it just happens. In a split second a flat poem can turn into a work of art by writing a word that appeared without warning. These are the creative moments provided by the divine inspiration of God through the Holy Spirit, and the supernatural invention of exceptional language is stunning in its creative impact. Therefore, a writer cannot rationally construct these thunderbolt words by themselves on demand. The Holy Spirit enables it to happen through holy involvement. If only the writer's physical involvement produced these types of other worldly words, then that same writer should be able to repeat such innovation and golden language whenever they wanted. Yet, they cannot because the illuminating power of figurative language is God's hand helping the writer through the Holy Spirit, and it does not occur by rational thought. It occurs by divine presence and prophesy. "For prophesy never had its origin in the will of man, but men spoke from God as they were carried along by the Holy Spirit" (2 Peter 1:21). In fact, the Holy Spirit is a writer's and everyone's intercessor to Jesus by making known Jesus' holy presence. "… but whatsoever he [the Holy Spirit] shall hear [from Jesus], that shall he speak: and he will shew you things to come" (John 16:13).

Once the Holy Spirit imparts divine language on a writer's work, thereafter a writer is always searching for more. It's like panning for gold in a creek bed and finding the first small shiny nugget. On one hand, it's an exhilarating experience for a writer, but then on the other hand the question becomes: I'm I going to find any more? Well, to a writer the answer to that question is maybe, if the writer invites the Holy Spirit's help. "With men this is impossible; but with God all things are possible" (Matthew 19:26). The Holy Spirit encourages a writer to continue to write by allowing the writer to experience positive writing feedback through these golden moments. In general, writers are restless people; they like to experiment with their own writing gifts for innovation. Some writers will write a novel and then the next time they will write a volume of poetry. Over time, most writers sense through the Holy Spirit that their talent often lies in only one genre. However, some writers are so gifted by God that they can write in many genres. For example, Robert Penn Warren was a gifted, multi-genre writer. Most home bookshelves should have Cleanth Brooks and Warren's textbook for English composition *Modern Rhetoric*, which I have used for writing advice for over 50 years; at least one collection of his many poetry volumes like *New and Selected Poems 1923-1985*, and several of his novels like *All the King's Men*. It's evident from Robert Penn Warren's diverse writing skills, especially in his poetry, that the Holy Spirit was at work in him. One of my favorite poems by Warren is *The Whistle of the 3 A.M.* because of its autobiographical roots. It's about a boy, maybe 8 or 9 years old, who rises from his bed on a winter's night to look out the window at a passing passenger train. Every night, the train whistle blows at 3 am at the town's crossing, and every night the boy rushes across the cold floorboards of his bedroom to reach the window to look at the train's passengers. Evidently, the train track is so close to his bedroom window that he can see the faces of the passengers and wonders where they are going. Then, the boy hopes that someday that he will be going somewhere on the train, too. But then, after the writer reminisces about this boyhood event, he wonders who today will remember a train's whistle at 3 am.

> Times change, man changes, and thirty-five thousand
>
> Feet down, what whistle wakes any boy
>
> To the world's bless and rage…?

In other words, no one even notices a jet carrying passengers at 35,000 feet. In short, society has lost a personal quality and now views life impersonally from a distance. Furthermore, in a subsequent poignant verse Warren asks who would even remember the <u>hope inspired</u> by the Holy Spirit of watching the close-up faces of passengers traveling by train? Most people who remember a train as a major form of US transportation have long since died. Thus, Robert Penn Warren uses this one boyhood autobiographical memory to remind the reader that life is short and that some things change but sooner or later we all will die.

> Who last remembers the 3 am?
>
> What if some hold real estate nearby,
>
> A good six feet long, but not one of them
>
> Would wake, I guess, to listen, and wonder why
>
> The schedule's gone dead of the 3 A.M.? (Warren 72)

So, the poem is about life and death, and our preoccupation with our own future. Yet, before we know it, our lives will also disappear like the train did on that winter's night.

Poetry, like Robert Penn Warren's *The Whistle at 3 A.M.,* is beautiful writing <u>guided</u> by the Holy Spirit to address a bigger moral question about life. While the poem is certainly

Robert Penn Warren's physical thinking, it is also the Holy Spirit interceding to wrap a moral lesson around an ordinary childhood memory. Thus, the Holy Spirit's presence becomes very evident in poetry because of poetry's brevity. There is a writer's adage: If you fail at becoming a poet, you become a short story writer. And if you fail at becoming a short story writer, you become a novelist. In other words, because a poet uses the least number of words to create, every word must carry great weight. Thus, poetry becomes both very exhalating for the poet to write, as well as exhilarating for the reader to read. Overall, writing poetry requires the self-determination of the poet along with the Holy Spirit's imagination to create and sustain the creative balance of writing in such a highwire environment. To be sure, for the Holy Spirit, all words exist in a vast cavern of creative hope, and this is especially true for poetry, where fewer words can create such beauty. "Out of your innermost being you shall flow… of the Spirit" (John 7:37).

Let's face it, writing can be very discouraging work when sometimes the imagistic words are just out of reach. Writers know when the "right" word is close by, but for some reason they still can't find it. I submit that finding the "right word" to use is as close as the Holy Spirit's proximity in your writing. In my case, sometimes the right word seems to be sitting right on the tip of my pen, yet I cannot find it, especially if I am only writing from the physical without the help of the Holy Spirit's energy. Then, at other times with the Holy Spirit's involvement in my writing, one word suddenly materializes out of nowhere, and it is so correct in its nuance and meaning that it glows like a precious stone. The brilliance of these words is a gift that comes from the Holy Spirit to the writer as wisdom. Wisdom is "… discernment, or insight" (*Random* 1500). Therefore, the Holy Spirit produces in us the spiritual qualities necessary to supply us with the evidence of God's work by judging rightly through discernment or insight. "But the fruit of the Spirit is love, joy, peace, longsuffering, gentleness, goodness, faith, meekness, temperance…" (Galatians 5:22-23). These are the spiritual qualities supplied by the Holy Spirit to see the world justly. Without them, writers will stumble around in the limited nature of their physical being because they do not pray to the Holy Spirit for <u>strength</u>, <u>direction</u>, and <u>encouragement</u> to escape their physical confinement. For them, the truth about the divine origins of their writing is lost and those bright and illuminating words will not be ultimately revealed. "But these signs [miracles] are written, that ye might believe that Jesus is the Christ, the Son of God; and that believing ye might have [holy] life through his name" (John 20:31).

Furthermore, the Holy Spirit's presence will also give a writer a greater sense of <u>purpose</u> about their writing. When the Holy Spirit's grants a sense of spiritual purpose to the writer and their work, the writer also experiences a <u>renewal</u> of their faith in their own writing ability and in their writing life. Jesus saved us from sin by renewing us. "Not by works of righteous that we have done but according to his mercy he saved us, by the washing of regeneration and renewing of the Holy Ghost" (Titus 3:5). Therefore, the Holy Spirit through Jesus offers the writer a <u>renewal</u> for both life's Spirit and enthusiasm for their writing. All work, no matter the kind, should include the divine inspiration of the Holy Spirit to sanction that work as holy. If allowed, the Lord Jesus through the Holy Spirit will walk with all laborers to produce joy and fruit from their efforts. And this includes writers who pray for the Holy Spirit's involvement in their work. "And we know that all things work together for good to them that love God, to them who are called according to his purpose" (Romans 8:28).

Let me ask you one question. Do you think that you were called (i.e., set aside) by God to be a writer? It's very important that you recognize and identify yourself as being a writer because writers who truly believe that they are on God's mission on earth will become better writers through the Holy Spirit. Being on a holy mission from God and using your God-given writing talents for His purpose is an awesome realization, and one responsibility that every writer should remember because writing is often lonely and unrewarding work. So why, if after so many writing disappointments and numerous writing setbacks, do you still write? The supernatural answer to that question is that you *must* write because God has ordained it for His purpose for your life. He gave you the gift of writing to be used for His holy intent, and the Holy Spirit knows you as a writer. Writing may be somewhat of a secular experience, but it originates from a spiritual one. Therefore, if God has called you to be a writer, you must now <u>trust</u> in Him to become one by seeking the <u>guidance</u> of the Holy Spirit. "Trust in the Lord will all thine heart; lean not unto thine own understanding" (Proverbs 3:5) In fact, those writers who do trust in the Lord Jesus' guidance through the Holy Spirit are writing from the heart of a prophet in the biblical tradition. True writers – as well as prophets -- have a <u>heartfelt belief</u> in the goodness of God to direct them as put there by Jesus and the Holy Spirit. They know that their talent for writing is a gift from God and that their talent does not stem from the secular world. It might be improved in the secular world through education, but their passion and talent for writing is deeply rooted in their being because it was put there by God, and it started long before their birth. They know that God has known them as a Spirit before they were born. They know that God knew them before He created the foundations of the world. They also know that He knew the when, where, and for what purpose they would be placed on the earth. "According as he hath chosen us in him before the foundation of the world, that we should be holy and without blame before him in love" (Ephesians 1:4). Therefore, as a writer you might have honed your writing skills in a university classroom, but your deep-rooted faith of becoming a writer was determined by God long before you were born. "And now, God has made known unto us the mystery of his will, according to his good pleasure" (Ephesians 1:9).

It's true that most writers will remain anonymous and unread, but God's will is still for the writer to write. God has His reasons for giving you the ability and determination to write. For example, my previous book, *Losing the Sound of Your Own Stride*, took 15 months to write, and during that time I thought that I'd have a couple of heart attacks. I spent thousands of hours writing and rewriting the manuscript without knowing whether it would ever be published. So why did I write the book? Why didn't I just stop? Well, frankly, I couldn't. I had to write the book because of the determination of the Holy Spirit within me. Frankly, I could not have written that book by myself. At times, the complex thought was almost too complicated for me to write; it took the Holy Spirit's involvement to <u>sustain</u> me. "And he that searcheth the hearts knoweth what is the mind of the Spirit, because he maketh intercession for the saints according to the will of God" (Romans 8:27). Thus, the <u>passion</u> for being a writer came from God's Holy Spirit before you were born, and a writer's <u>endurance</u> to improve as a writer and a person while on earth while weathering the undulations of life is also provided by the Holy Spirit. "Make me to understand the way of thy precepts: so shall I talk of thy wonderous works" (Palm 119:27).

Questions

1. Do you believe that you are a writer?
2. What inspires you to write?
3. Why do you continue to write despite setbacks?
4. Name three pieces of writing inspired by your autobiographical roots.

Essay 5 The Writing Stage and the Holy Spirit

For most writers, the writing stage follows the prewriting stage. This is when the writer becomes the <u>prophet</u> of their own thinking because their planning becomes a prediction about what will take place in their writing's future. By planning with the help of the Holy Spirit, a writer predicts that future writing will take place. Therefore, a writer through the Holy Spirit is a seer of future things before their thoughts become realized into words (e.g., Mozart). To a writer, the silent void between the planning stage and the writing stage echoes loudly. It's when the writer first stares at a blank page without yet writing the first word. Writing the first word of any piece of writing is the most difficult, and it takes the most thought and courage. In this hollow space between planning and writing, the Holy Spirit creates substantive <u>vision and courage</u> for the writer to begin. By staring at the first blank page and then turning it from one word into substantial pages, a writer -- like a prophet -- embarks on a perilous journey to predict an outcome in the future. Some writers look at a blank page for weeks before proclaiming their intention by writing their first word. And during that time, many good writers are praying and waiting for the Holy Spirit to give them <u>inspiration</u> to get started.

One time, it took me thirty-two years to finish the third verse of a country song. The song's title was *Wake Me From This Nightmare*, and I couldn't finish it because the Holy Spirit wasn't with me. So, for me it was indeed a 32-year personal nightmare. Then, one day I wrote the missing third verse in 5 minutes. Ironically, the third verse that was created by the involvement of the Holy Spirit turned out to be a spiritual verse and the answer to a man's dilemma regarding a lost love. The lines from the third verse provided by the Holy Spirit created a spiritual note of <u>wisdom</u> in the song that my mind did not expect. The man in the song meets his lost love for the first time after their breakup, and she's riding in an expensive new car being driven by another man. So, here's the third verse description of the scene and the car as written by the Holy Spirit:

Half a block long and big wide tires,

Pulling up the Cemetery Ridge at half-passed a choir.

Two- lane blacktop stretching out for miles,

And she rolled down her window at him and slowly smiled.

At the last line's "slowly smiled," it became evident to me that the song was about why the woman had left the man. She had left him for material possessions, and at that point the song then took on a new spiritual meaning because it provided the listeners with the woman's insidious smile as evidence of her sinful behavior. "For the love of money is the root of all evil" (Timothy 6:10) Suddenly, the Holy Spirit had not only helped me to finish the lyrics of the song, but the Holy Spirit also strengthened me in my <u>weakness</u> to find the lyrics to finish the song. Now, the Holy Spirit had given me a spiritual reason for the song to exist. I had no idea that the song would turn into a spiritual statement about the love of money and how that would be a theme in the song lyric, but the Holy Spirit did! Furthermore, I started writing *Wake Me For This Nightmare* in the fall of 1974, and I didn't finish it until in the spring of 2006, although it was not for a lack of trying. For some reason during those 32 years, I kept humming the melody, and I tried unsuccessfully many times to finish the lyrics. Now, I know that I was supposed to hum the song's melody for 32 years until the Holy Spirit's arrival to finish the song for me. Furthermore, it is also significant that I started that song before I knew the Lord Jesus as my personal Lord and Savior and that the song lyric wasn't completed until after Jesus had granted me His gift of salvation. This parallel experience between receiving the saving grace of Jesus Christ coinciding with my song's spiritual completion alerted me to the fact that writing through the Holy Spirit is a <u>sanctifying experience</u>. Writing brings one closer to Jesus to be more like him. In this case, the Holy Spirit wrote the third verse lyrics, and it brought me closer to Jesus. Furthermore, it brought closure to a very unsettling experience in my life. You see, I was the man in the song who had experienced the heartache of lost love, and I wrote that song initially to get some closure on an unsettling event, but no closure ever happened until the Holy Spirit intervened 32 years later to finish the song. Additionally, the story about the missing song lyrics written by the Holy Spirit doesn't end there. The Holy Spirit directed me to a recording studio, and I recorded the song because the Holy Spirit had finished it so beautifully, and it rose on the European Country Music Chart to #26 in Norway and #31 in Sweden. So, the Holy Spirit's involvement in my autobiographical song about my own lost love experience must have resonated and healed someone else's broken heart in Scandinavia. I must admit that throughout the 32 years that the song remained unfinished, I wrote hundreds of secular endings to it but none of them seemed right. For example, the estranged couple could have reconciled. The new boyfriend could have left her. The car could have had a flat tire. The protagonist could have turned to whiskey to console himself. But no ending for the song seemed appropriate until the Holy Spirit provided one because Jesus wanted a sacred song lyric to end my own unsettled misery about an unpleasant experience. Ultimately, the song with a spiritual message helped others, but it also helped me to accept Jesus as my Lord and Savior and to accept the Holy Spirit's involvement in my writing. For the record (no pun intended), the Holy Spirit is not listed at BMI as the co-writer for the song, although in truth every song ever written is God inspired.

Questions

1. What is the longest time that you've worked on a piece of writing?
2. Is the length of time that it takes to finish a piece of writing important?
3. Who sustains a writer when a piece of writing seemingly takes forever?
4. Who finally directs you to finish that piece of writing?

Essay 6 Patience is Supplied by the Holy Spirit

After some substantial planning, most writers believe that placing at least one word on the page will also be forthcoming. But to write well, a writer must have _patience_ supplied by the Holy Spirit. Patience is a commodity that most people lack. The world is in a fast-paced, moral freefall under Satan's control. It is a fast-paced and chaotic mess because Satan wants it that way. Satan doesn't want you to slow down to think. He just wants you to keep moving in your secular life without regard for your spiritual health. Of course, if you work too hard and think too little, then life passes too quickly, which makes Satan happy because in your quest to acquire secular things like money and power, you have completely forgotten about nurturing your own Spirit. In most occupations, the secular world controlled by Satan promotes ruthless schedules. For example, the college textbook publishing industry is totally schedule-driven. College textbook production demands perfection from multiple people to perform their part of a book's production to meet the schedule on time. If any part of a book's production schedule is unmet, it jeopardizes the publication date for the book by "end loading" or possibly delaying the project. For instance, if the art illustrators do not have the artwork at least sized for every book page, then it threatens the production schedule for typesetting the first page proofs. So, throughout the book production process, a cause-and-effect relationship exists among all departments, and a high level of cooperation and efficiency is demanded throughout the college textbook production process. Therefore, the business world does not honor patience; instead, it honors impatience and efficiency. The adage "I need it yesterday" has corrupted the world from finding its soul. Of course, production efficiency requires controlling the variables to create an environment that maximizes productivity. Some writers practice a personal version of this production efficiency by giving themselves an artificial page quota to complete each day. As mentioned previously, Stephen King wanted to write six pages per day, which was a self-imposed schedule that reassured him about making progress. Ernest Hemingway wanted to write ten good pages per day. Many authors use this page-quota-per-day of writing as a way of keeping themselves on schedule. Yet only the Holy Spirit <u>empowers</u> us to write and ensures us that we will complete the work. The Holy Spirit guides our writing as a service to God and <u>enables</u> us to find the patience to complete our work in our specific calling." ... but we glory in tribulations also: knowing that tribulation worketh patience; And patience, experience, and experience, hope...because the love of God is shed abroad in our hearts by the Holy Ghost which is given unto us" (Romans 5:3-5).

For a writer, patience is essential, although the real world doesn't teach much of it. Therefore, the writer must learn to get their <u>patience</u> from the Holy Spirit. In fact, the Holy Spirit tells a writer when to be inspired to write and when not to be inspired. Starting to write solely in your physical self without the Holy Spirit's supernatural energy is a bad idea because the Holy Spirit gathers the supernatural energy necessary and gives it to a writer in the form of <u>inspiration</u> to begin. The word *inspiration* comes from the Latin word *inspirare*, which means "to breath into or fill with breath or spirit." The <u>patience</u> given to a writer before they write as well as having the <u>energy,</u> <u>strength,</u> and <u>enthusiasm</u> to write are all given by the Holy Spirit. The word *enthusiasm* comes from the Greek adjective *enthros*, meaning "having God within." It is in the <u>passion</u> of this single moment when the impulse to write and doing it occurs that the Holy Spirit imparts the <u>courage</u> to begin. Writers do not decide when to write; the Holy Spirit decides. Writers who can feel the Holy Spirit working on them know the precise moment at which to begin to write. They can feel and sense the sacredness of that moment when the Holy Spirit stirs their creative heart. As mentioned previously, when Mozart wrote a piece of music, he thought about it for a long period of time. Yet, when he finally wrote the music, his biographer, Alfred Einstein reported, "All witnesses of Mozart at work agree that he put a composition down on paper as one writes a letter, without allowing any disturbance or interruption to annoy him, the writing down, the fixing was nothing more than that –the fixing of a completed work, a mechanical act" (Gardner 358-60). Therefore, once Mozart began to write, it was a mechanical process rather than a creative one that produced an almost flawless finish product. Who supplied Mozart with these near flawless music compositions in his brain? Of course, it was the Holy Spirit. The musical compositions came from beyond Mozart to him when the Holy Spirit imparted the wisdom of music.

As every writer knows, planning to write in your mind and actually doing the writing are two different things. Some people who profess to be writers never write. Their procrastination is understandable because writing is such a difficult journey down multiple paths with multiple setbacks. It takes both <u>courage</u> and <u>boldness</u> to become a writer. Of course, it doesn't happen overnight because it takes the maturation of the writer's awareness of the Holy Spirit to sustain the strength, resolve, and commitment to learn and improve continually. In fact, many people attribute being courageous and bold as personality traits befitting writers. In truth, writers are tenacious people, but they need to be tenacious to be any good at writing. Yet all writers must never forget that the Holy Spirit grants them those gifts to use for God's purpose." And when they had prayed, the place was shaken where they were assembled together; and they were all filled with the Holy Ghost, and they spake the word of God with boldness" (Acts 4:31).

In addition, writers usually have personalities of an inquisitive nature given to them by the Holy Spirit because the very act of writing demands curiosity. Being a writer means having an inquisitive nature and a thirst for finding the truth. This type of personality has a penchant for asking questions. And asking questions takes the boldness of Spirit and the courage to find and accept the answers. In fact, the Holy Spirit gives the writer their strength to exhibit that boldness in their commitment to find the truth. To do this, the Holy Spirit gives a writer the Spirit of conviction to put one sincere word on the page after another in search of the truth. Therefore, the boldness necessary to be a writer comes from the Holy Spirit. Think about the boldness necessary to be an investigative newspaper reporter. Think about international journalists who risk their lives every day by traveling to war zones to report the news, or a crime novelist who visits a dangerous drug cartel city because a chapter in their novel demands greater accuracy? In fact, I once asked a famous writer why he always carried a 38-revolver handgun? He responded, "So I can go anywhere I want." In truth, the early writers of the Gospel of Jesus received that same boldness from the Holy Spirit to spread the Word. They, too, needed the strength of the Holy Spirit's conviction within them to write Jesus' message about truth and love. Even writers with timid personalities are sometimes emboldened to action by the Holy Spirit's power. Again, think about the courage of war correspondents right now in the Ukraine who risk their lives to record for the world what is happening in the war. No rational person would purposely head into a war zone like in Ukraine to write; it takes a person filled with the Holy Spirit's conviction and courage to be there and write the truth. "The Holy Spirit sovereignly bestows spiritual gifts or abilities for service to every believer" (Ephesians 4). In contrast, Satan is incapable of telling any truth, and he certainly doesn't want a writer to reveal it. So, when writers expose evil by writing the truth, they follow the Holy Spirit's energy <u>to produce the fruit</u> of their calling.

Questions

1. Are you a patient person?
2. How can you become more patient?
3. Why is it important for a writer to be patient?
4. Are you by nature a curious person?

Essay 7 Rough Draft, Writing Styles, and the Holy Spirit

Many of the words written in the rough draft will not be found in the final draft. This is because nothing is ever perfect the first time in either life or in writing. In some ways, life's experiences must be mirrored in a writer's experience. For example, surviving and improving in life requires praying to Jesus for insight to learn from past mistakes. Likewise, learning how to copyedit your own writing to delete past mistakes is essential to improve the work. Therefore, adaptation is the key to improvement in both life and writing; and in both realms the Holy Spirit's guidance is essential for survival.

A rough draft's content is usually written quickly in a fast-and-furious writing style that advances information without fanfare. The diction (i.e., word choice) is often flawed and void of spiritual import. Kurt Vonnegut once described two types of writing styles, and in some ways these two types of writing styles mirror the differences between writing the rough draft and writing a polished final draft. In Kurt Vonnegut's novel *TimeQuake*, Vonnegut classifies writers into two groups: *bashers* and *swoopers*. Bashers plan before they write. "… [they] go one sentence at a time, getting it exactly right before they go on to the next one." They write in a heavy-handed style like they are sledgehammering each letter into place. There is nothing delicate or artful about a basher's writing style; it is straightforward, planned, and to-the-point communication. Some of the gumshoe mystery novelists of the 1940-1950's had a basher's writing style with short sentence structures and clipped diction to exemplify hard-nosed characters (e.g., "just the facts"). Bashers use words like tools to construct meaning according to a blueprint. By contrast, the swooper writer writes a story quickly to see what happens, and "…..then they go over it again painstakingly, fixing everything that doesn't work"(Davis). In my opinion, a swooper has a more artistic writing style because it relies less on human reasoning in the rough draft. When choosing words, they swoop in quickly to transfer information delicately through numerous and colorful descriptive adjectives and adverbs. In addition, swooper writers tend to use long sentences. When I think of swooper writers, I think of Henry James, who wrote two incredible novels *The American* and *The Ambassadors* in a long-winded style. In fact, many critics, including Oscar Wilde and Henry Adams, said of James' long sentence writing style that "he chewed more than he bit off" thus implying that he was successful in a long-winded way. For instance, the first few pages of his novel *The Ambassadors* contains only a few very long, long sentences, sometimes approaching 100 words or more. So why would James do this to a reader, especially when statistically most average reading comprehension begins to lose meaning after the 27th word in a sentence? Why would James intentionally make his writing style so long and difficult for most readers? Well, as a swooper by writing longer sentences he was putting the reader on notice. He was implying to the reader, "Try to keep up with me, if you can." Accordingly, the swooper writer's sentences are purposely and artfully lengthy and contain many descriptive details dropping from 40,000 feet to reach the reader's eye in a split second.

George RR Martin, author of *The Game of Thrones*, also describes two types of writers: the architects and the gardeners. The Architects plan everything before they start. Everything is designed and blueprinted before time. The gardener plants a seed, not knowing exactly how it will grow. As the writer progresses, it sprouts here and there, taking on different directions" (Davis).

In addition, Henry James' novel *The American* is an excellent example of how a theme in a novel can be a moral lesson to the reader as inspired by the Holy Spirit. In *The*

American, James uses the social status of his characters to advance a moral message about money. The novel takes place at the turn of the century during America's Industrial Revolution after The Civil War. The United States Industrial Revolution created many overnight American millionaires who created products that all Americans needed and wanted. In *The American*, I believe that the protagonist made millions of dollars by manufacturing toilet seats. Consequently, the *nouveau riche* in America often felt that common people in America weren't good enough for them to marry, so they traveled to Europe to find a suitable mate by buying sophistication with marrying into royalty. However, when many new millionaires from America arrived in Europe to find and court a European aristocrat, not many aristocrats would marry a crass American businessman. At that time in Europe, the aristocrats had fallen on desperate economic times, and their castles were crumbling into ruins predicated by England's own rising industrial class and its newfound power. So, after traveling abroad, it was difficult for an astute American businessman to understand why a poor European aristocrat wouldn't want to marry a rich American industrialist. But the financially broke European aristocrats still had their pride, even if they no longer had their money. They didn't want to advance the notion that newly acquired money was equal to their old money and royal bloodline, so many of them didn't want to accommodate a crass American's businessman's pursuit of marrying into royalty. By the end of the novel, despite all the overtures and courtship, the aristocratic woman who the crass American millionaire wants to marry enters a convent instead of marrying him. Thus, in one of the novel's final scenes the American businessman is standing outside the convent separated from his European marital prospect by a high stone wall, symbolizing the impenetrable separation of social classes. It is also significant that the European woman chooses to marry God rather than him. Of The American,

Henry James said, "we are each the product of circumstances and there are stone walls which fatally divide us" (Edel).

Most poetic writers –that is, those who write to seek the greatest audience possible-- begin to write because they want to create something meaningful to be read. Many times, the novice poetic writer will at first bash forward in a heavy-handed style that bulldozes words into place. But after some writing practice and experience, some bashers lighten their touch with words and begin to understand that writing is a sacred act given to them by God. For good writers, words become like chess piece movements where small, graceful improvements add up to a collective artful whole. There's a vast difference between someone "slashing" the shrubbery and someone "pruning" it. In fact, good writers don't really write words; they dance with them with the Holy Spirit as their partner.

Kurt Vonnegut wrote a wonderful short story about art and dancing titled *Harrison Bergeron*. The story takes place in a futuristic society where the US government employs a Handicapper General to place heavy lead weights and sandbags on ballet dancers who can jump higher and are more graceful than other dancers. The point to these heavy weights is to make all ballet dancers equal in ability. In the opening scene of the story, a perfectly normal middle-aged man is sitting in his living room watching television. He is watching Harrison Bergeron, a ballet dancer, and Bergeron and his partner were swirling like no other dancers could. When this point about the unequal gracefulness of the dancers on tv was about to be made by the man to his wife, a great sound like a head-on car crash enters his brain and scatters his thoughts, thus eliminating his unequal thoughts about how beautiful the dance was being performed. The car crash in the man's head drove the inequality about life from his thoughts. Well, it appears that Harrison Bergeron, the male dancer, was so much better than the other ballet dancers that the Handicapper General had weighted him down with so many handicaps that he looked like a "walking junkyard." Lead weights and sandbags hung all over him. Yet, even with these handicaps, he could still outperform other dancers, which made him in the government's eyes a very dangerous man because he was being unequal. In the last scene of the short story, while still dancing on television, Harrison rips off his handicaps "like tissue paper" as well as his partner's handicaps, and they danced "like deer on the moon." At this point in the story, the Government's Handicapper General barges through the tv studio doors and shoots them both dead with a 12-gauge shotgun (Vonnegut). I guess the inequality of artistic expression is unacceptable to some people.

Of course, it's a story about artists, in general, who by their God-given talents vary in their abilities for artistic expression. Individual expression is the whole point to becoming an artist. People write, paint, sculp, or dance because the Holy Spirit helps them to <u>express themselves uniquely</u>, and to make all artistic expression artificially equal is absurd. In many ways artistic expression fuses across all artforms. For example, when a good writer who listens through the Holy Spirit to the sound of their words, the syllables become musical notes, the tone becomes a melody, and the sentence variety becomes a cadence like a drummer's tempo. All artistic endeavors are connected because of the Holy Spirit's possibility of creative <u>promise</u>. In the short story *Harrison Bergeron* that artistic promise is being silenced by the government.

The Holy Spirit also makes creating <u>fun</u> for a writer, and most truthful writers know that they are not working alone, whether they admit it or not. All works of art contain some hint of <u>originality</u>, which is unexpectedly given to the writer by the Holy Spirit. "God is a Spirit: and they that worship him must worship him in the spirit and in truth" (John 4:25). Most fiction and nonfiction writers are surprised by at least one creative point in every work that they did not expect because it came from somewhere else and not from them. Ironically, it is that one creative nugget derived from the Holy Spirit's involvement that <u>encourages</u> the writer to continue to write. All writer's inspiration to create comes as a gift from the Holy Spirit. In addition, the Holy Spirit offers writers the <u>will</u> and <u>determination</u> to continue, even without being published or without favorable book reviews. Thus, despite daunting setbacks, writers continue their work with the Holy Spirit's <u>encouragement</u>. By helping the writer to recognize the value of their own creative efforts, the Holy Spirit verifies the real reason why any person writes— because it was willed to them to do so by God! Therefore, The Holy Spirit creates a <u>sacred awareness</u> in a writer. Feeling the beauty of language can't be taught; it must be felt and honored from the heart through the Holy Spirit's involvement. So, it appears that writers can start as a basher and end up as a swooper as they improve their writing on God's continuous improvement plan. Or they can also (as in the case of rushing to meet a publication deadline) start as a swooper and end up a basher depending on the deadline and genre of writing.

However, there is a third option that the Holy Spirit places into a writer's heart that creates a hybrid basher-swooper combination. This combination contains the instincts of both basher and swooper. Hybrid writers are usually professional writers who use both sides of their brain and know when to use which side. Professional writers have both basher left brain tendencies and swooper right brain instincts, yet they also know that the Holy Spirit is in <u>control of both of them</u> and directing them about which side of their brain to use. In short, the Holy Spirit tells them when to bash and when to swoop. In these cases, readers know that a person is a "gifted" writer because the Holy Spirit provides the <u>gift</u> of genius. Although the word *genius* is much used, geniuses are rare. A genius can be defined as using both sides of their brain to create. For instance, through the Holy Spirit a genius can intuitively sense when being a swooper or basher is better. However, to work properly, the writer must first release their own ego and allow the Holy Spirit to participate, which gives a writer this insight. It is a supernatural phenomenon when writers find themselves writing from someplace beyond themselves when the Holy Spirit interprets their writing from the heart. The Holy Spirit moves these experienced writers gracefully from one side of their brain to the other to create a whole brain experience. Psychologists define this whole brain writing experience as being relational to being a genius. Therefore, with the Holy Spirit's direction, the hybrid professional writer can move back and forth across their brain hemispheres to provide the best possible whole brain writing experience for the reader. In literary terms, this is when the writing is so good that it takes the reader from their own reality into the reality of the author's imagination, which is provided by the Holy Spirit. Writers are capable of shaping the unifying parts of a story into a unified whole by the emotional commitment to their writing supplied by the Holy Spirit. Therefore, when to be a basher or a swooper is a supernatural choice and not a rational one. It is the writer's emotional involvement provided by the Holy Spirit that connects and combines all the pieces of their chaotic life into one sure passionate, autobiographical account. Therefore, it is the Holy Spirit's passion being passed to the writer that is the "glue" that holds the writer's thoughts together so that a purpose for writing can surface. In short, the Holy Spirit gives a writer the passionate feeling to write about something important to them. And that passionate feeling is transferred from the Holy Spirit to a writer and then to a writer's story. Subsequently, the writer's ability to recognize the Holy Spirit's control on their writing helps a writer to improve by learning how to adjust from basher brain to swooper brain. In fact, many experienced writers know when they're shifting brain hemispheres from using one type of writing to another and whether it requires left or right brain thinking.

I know that tracking your own thought process while writing sounds a little crazy. But those writers who can sense the Holy Spirit's <u>direction</u> for their writing can also sense how, when, and why the Holy Spirit is moving them. For example, I wrote a science fiction novella, *The Last Chord Concert*, in 7 four-hour writing sessions. And during that time, I literally caught myself understanding the writing process of shifting from the left and right brain through the Holy Spirit's directives. Sometimes, I caught myself saying aloud, "And now, it's time to shift to the right brain for description" as I followed the Holy Spirit's <u>instruction</u>. I was blessed to write the entire book in this manner. "But you shall receive power when the Holy Spirit has come upon you…" (Acts 1:8).

Questions

1. Why should a writer understand their writing style?
2. What kinds of literary elements define a writing style?
3. Can a writing style change with gaining writing experience?
4. Why is understanding left and right brain dominance important to a writer?

Essay 8 The Holy Spirit Elevates Meaning

Any attempt to write is a good start because some words are now written on the page that weren't there before, and there must be at least one "keeper" word among the bunch. The writer is writing in the rough draft stage to put as many words on the page as possible. Experienced writers will tell you that the rough draft stage also includes a great temptation to sidetrack the writer by editing at the same time while they write. In short, the writer is tempted to stop, backup, and correct small errors at the same time when they are trying to write and develop larger thoughts. I believe that this disruption of large thoughts by small elements is Satan's doing. By distracting the writer from initiating larger thoughts and moving writing forward in favor of correcting smaller ones, Satan is trying to block the writer's progress. Writing and editing are two separate stages in the writing process, and Satan interrupts the writing of important thoughts to correct a misspelled word to distract the writer from the more important mission of putting important thoughts on the page. The Holy Spirit's creative advice for creating larger and more important thoughts can disappear in a fraction of a second, although an already written misspelled word will always be there to correct. It's so like Satan to distract the writer from seeking what's important in both life and in writing. In fact, Satan's world is all about distraction and deception. Therefore, important thoughts supplied by the Holy Spirit should always be captured and written first. I used the word "captured" because good thoughts are elusive as squirrels. A writer just can't run up to a good thought and expect to pick it up, no matter how cute it might be. In fact, creative good thoughts are trained to behave by the Holy Spirit; they either come to you when summoned or they don't, depending on how much the Holy Spirit is involved in your writing. In essence, the Holy Spirit gifts the writer important thought. That's why some writers sit at their desk day after day staring at a blank computer screen and never writing a thought. I submit that the thoughts that they seek are still hidden at the top their mind, where they can only be coaxed down into their consciousness by the Holy Spirit.

As mentioned previously, the rough draft stage is used to write words and to move thoughts forward by the <u>determination</u> of the Holy Spirit without backing up to pay attention to smaller errors like misspelled words, incorrect punctuation, or sentence structure, etc. In writing classes, there are exercises to undo the ingrained habit of trying to write and edit at the same time. One classic classroom exercise to undo the habit of trying to write and edit at the same time is called *free writing*, where a student focuses on getting words on the page without backing up to edit them. The free writing exercise involves writing for ten minutes without stopping. Once the pen or pencil hits the page, the writer does not stop or look back. The point is to get the student to write while <u>moving forward</u> with the Holy Spirit without thinking about moving backwards with Satan to edit. Some educators call free writing "babbling on paper" because the writer just writes about what comes into their mind. What you write doesn't have to make sense; making sense doesn't matter. The point is to move the words forward by writing thoughts that occur moment by moment in your mind over a ten-minute period. For example, a free write might read: "I like peanut butter. Fishhooks are great. Can you swim? Going to the basketball game tonight." By not worrying about things like grammar, sentences, punctuation, mechanics, or content, a writer <u>moves</u> with the Holy Spirit to the center of the writing lane and establishes guardrails for writing forward and not editing backward. Without the Holy Spirit establishing guardrails that separate the writing stage from the rewriting (editing) stage, a writer will burn more time correcting little mistakes provided by Satan than moving big thoughts ahead provided by the Holy Spirit. A good thought might not be there in a moment, but the small written error will be. Therefore, the rough draft should concentrate on <u>generating thought</u> and <u>creative</u> <u>ideas</u> through the Holy Spirit that can later be refined in the copyediting/ rewriting stage. If you stop a good thought to backup and correct a comma, it's like stopping your car on an eight-lane expressway to pick up a penny. It's dangerous to pursue small things at great risk. Once the Holy Spirit's <u>encourages</u> a writer to start, take advantage of the <u>holy gift</u> of finally beginning and write forward.

Many writers are very disappointed in the quality of their first rough draft, yet unfortunately they seem to be very satisfied with the quality of their rough draft life. Statistically, people remember bad things for 10 times longer than they remember good things, and this includes bad things about themselves. In effect, writers often try to write and edit their own lives at the same time, while wasting time to reflect needlessly about their past mistakes, which they cannot change, while God and Jesus through the Holy Spirit are trying to <u>write forward</u> the next chapter of their current life. While every writer should see their own life as a rough draft to be improved, inordinate dwelling on past mistakes is unhealthy both in writing and in life because it is often a useless waste of energy. All writers should learn from their past mistakes but spending an inordinate amount of time living in the past instead of living in the present to change the future is not healthy and is Satan's idea. Therefore, looking backward instead of moving forward is a mistake in both writing and in life.

The Holy Spirit was sent by Jesus to <u>comfort</u> us in times of despair. Therefore, a writer who does not seek comfort in the Holy Spirit from sin is probably overly preoccupied with things of the flesh. The flesh cannot move your life or your writing forward because both take the supernatural power of Jesus.

The Holy Spirit works these gifts in us for the profit of all. "But the manifestation of the Spirit is given to every man to profit withal. For to one is given by the Spirit the word of wisdom; to another the word of knowledge by the same Spirit; To another faith by the same Spirit; to another the gifts of healing by the same Spirit" (1 Corinthians 12: 7-9). Therefore, a writer must become <u>enlightened spiritually</u> by the Holy Spirit's <u>promptings</u>. Without the supernatural guidance of God through Jesus and the Holy Spirit, a writer can do nothing. "I am the vine, ye are the branches: He that abideth in me, and I in him, the same bringeth forth much fruit: for without me ye can do nothing" (John 15:5). Therefore, when a writer's life becomes just a physical space instead of a spiritual place, they lose the Holy Spirit's comfort and guidance. Most of life's problems have spiritual origins, and a writer living in a rough draft life by relying solely on themselves to write and live needs the <u>help</u> and <u>comfort</u> of the Holy Spirit to improve. In short, how can a life lived in the flesh solve a problem found in the Spirit?

Questions

1. What should a writer be doing in the rough draft stage?
2. Why is it important for a writer to focus on writing thoughts forward?
3. When you stop writing forward, what happens to your thoughts?
4. Are writing and editing two separate processes?

Essay 9 The Holy Spirit's Guidance

A few weeks ago, I retired from a lifelong teaching career in higher education. On my last day of teaching, the Holy Spirit prompted me to recall the interview for my first full-time college teaching job. I applied for a job in Iowa to teach College Composition and other writing courses. At the job interview, I was asked if besides teaching writing courses if I could also teach a course in 17th Century British Literature? I couldn't teach British Literature; I wasn't trained to do it. I was trained to teach writing. My MA was in the teaching of English composition and grammar. Consequently, I was blindsided by the question; the job posting didn't say anything about teaching literature, but I needed the job, so I signed a two-year teaching contract. I then drove 500 miles home to Michigan. On the drive home, I was terrified about not being able to teach the literature class, but I had the entire month of August to prepare. For three weeks, I roamed a large university library without success at finding any materials about how to teach the course. I had exhausted all the sources in the library's databases without any success. Then one day in late August out of desperation, I just started walking aimlessly around the library in the hopes of finding something. For an unknown reason, I climbed the staircase to the fourth floor where the biology books were shelved, and for another unknown reason, I walked over to a bookshelf labelled Biomedicine, looked up, and found a misplaced and unregistered book with the library's computer database on *How to Teach 17th Century British Literature*. For some reason, the book had remained unrecorded in the library's computer system. At the time, I felt both relieved and grateful. Yet, this was before I knew the Lord, so I didn't know who to thank for my good fortune. Today, on my last day of college teaching while writing this book, the Holy Spirit prompted me to open my eyes as to who I had to thank. Namely, Jesus. Jesus had the Holy Spirit guide me to that bookshelf in the library to find the elusive unrecorded and misplaced book that I so desperately needed. Today, I still feel bad about lying to the job interviewer about being able to teach 17th Century British Literature, lying has never been one of my personality traits. Perhaps Jesus rewarded me with the book because the job posting failed to mention teaching a literature course as a requirement, and I had driven 500 miles to the interview in good faith. I certainly don't think that Jesus Christ rewards liars, although on that day when I found that book no rational explanation seems plausible. But one thing is for sure: that book found me! I did not find it.

Questions

1. Can you recall some event in your life that you can't explain?
2. Can everything in life be explained by facts and reasons?
3. Are there supernatural forces at work in your life?
4. What supernatural forces provide the writer comfort?

Essay 10 The Holy Spirit's Rough Draft Guidance

    Writers should prepare to write by first praying to Jesus for the Holy Spirit's <u>help</u>. "And I will ask the father, and he will give you another Helper, to be with you forever" (John 14:16). Therefore, the Holy Spirit is involved in even the most mundane daily tasks. Praying to Jesus and the Holy Spirit to join you in your writing effort will also move you closer to your Spiritual self and your writing potential. Preparing to write is a Holy Spirit-inspired act because the ritualistic preparations are designed to <u>produce fruit</u>. If you're a writer, being fruitful means writing more and writing better. In short, by embracing the <u>fellowship</u> of the Holy Spirit's insight both in the way a writer lives and writes, a writer can move closer to their own Spirit, closer to their own redemption through Jesus' gift of salvation, and closer to their writing potential. "That which we have seen and heard declare we unto you, that ye also may have fellowship with us: and truly our fellowship is with the Father, and with his Son Jesus Christ" (1 John 1:3). By having fellowship and being "reborn" in the Spirit through Jesus Christ, the rough draft stage for a writer's life ends and a new reborn spiritually powered writer emerges. Those writers who live for Jesus through their Holy Spirit know that their <u>creativity</u> comes from supernatural involvement. Even at their creative best, writers need Jesus and the Holy Spirit's assistance to improve and to make every word count. "Now we have received, not the spirit of the world, but the spirit which is of God: that we might know the things that are freely given to us of God" (1 Corinthians 2:12). Therefore, penning a masterpiece during the rough draft stage is nearly impossible both on the page and in life, although God did it when He etched the Ten Commandments in stone with one finger in one draft. As far as I know, this is the only occurrence of a perfect first draft.

Therefore, most writers know that writing done in the rough draft is merely a rough resemblance of the final product; it crudely resembles what it might be with further revisions. Overall, most first drafts get better by the Holy Spirit <u>releasing power</u> to the writer by supplying the writer with copyediting <u>guidance</u> and <u>patience</u>. As Kurt Vonnegut once said, "Another flaw in the human character is that everybody wants to build and nobody wants to do maintenance" (Hocus Pocus 167)." Well, copyediting is like doing maintenance on your rough draft. It isn't easy; it isn't pretty; it isn't often creative, but it must be done. Wouldn't it be nice if we could just observe writing over a good writer's shoulder and become a good writer the first time ourselves? But we can't, so most writers do what they can to improve their own work. Writers who are serious about the craft are also avid readers; by reading better writers they become better writers themselves. In this regard, the Holy Spirit <u>guides</u> a writer to read certain books by authors who will improve their work. For instance, if you want a good example about how to write more believable characterizations, read Charles Dickens' *Great Expectations.* Thus, for thousands of years previous writers have had an influence on current writers. It is God's gift to them. In this instance, the Holy Spirit <u>intercedes</u> on a writer's behalf to guide them in how to improve. God created gifted authors for their readers to enjoy and to learn more about themselves and life. In fact, the Bible is the best example of reading for self-improvement. "All scripture is given by inspiration of God and is profitable for doctrine, for reproof, for correction, and for instruction in righteousness" (2 Timothy 3:16). Some people allude to the Bible as <u>The Instruction Manual for Life</u> because it contains the information about how to live life according to God's purpose.

Henry David Thoreau's quote "Men lead lives of quiet desperation" is a classic example of how the Holy Spirit imparts to an author the <u>wisdom</u> of <u>vision and moral purpose</u> for writing by arriving at an eternal moral <u>truth</u>. By Thoreau building a log cabin on *Walden Pond* through the <u>guidance</u> of the Holy Spirit and removing himself from society, he was able to observe the chaos of economic and social disorder of his surroundings. In fact, Thoreau's moral message recorded in his journal was so astute that it transcends time because it reflects a basic human condition that has remained throughout history. Thoreau's moral lesson, and one that remains with us today, is that putting your faith in acquiring possessions and in other people for your meaning in life is futile. For as long as people put their trust in physical things and in other people instead of in Jesus, they will continue to feel the emptiness of a "quiet desperation" in their lives. Thus, only through a <u>spiritual awakening</u> in Jesus through the Holy Spirit can that feeling of desperation be quelled.

Thoreau's observations written in his journal on *Walden Pond* states a moral truth. By replacing living a shallow, spiritually disconnected life based on economic gain with an individual life based on gaining greater spiritual understanding, the Holy Spirit was influencing Thoreau to embrace a basic truth that spiritual wellbeing is far more important that secular wellbeing. In life, the Holy Spirit provides that <u>comfort</u> and <u>direction</u> to find moral truth for a writer. Thus, in my opinion, *Walden Pond* was inspired by the Holy Spirit because it addresses the importance of preserving the integrity of the Soul in a world temporarily overwhelmed by the secular influences of Satan. In short, Thoreau's *Walden Pond* speaks to the soul of the reader about its own importance (Thoreau). "And let us not be weary in well doing: for in due season we shall reap. If we faint not" (Galatians 6:9).

Therefore, in any rough draft stage -- whether in life or writing -- writers need the Holy Spirit's <u>vision</u> because they are openly admitting that both could be better with more time and practice. In one case, it is the improvement of writing, but in another case of life it is understanding their holy significance by praying to Jesus and feeling the Holy Spirit's power working in them. By discerning the Holy Spirit's power working in them, writers can sense an acute awareness regarding the Holy Spirit's <u>vision </u>for the direction of their work. Whether a character performs this action or that action is determined by the writer with the <u>help</u> of the Holy Spirit. In fact, one of the Holy Spirit's major gifts to a writer is the gift of judgement based on <u>discernment.</u> "Discernment is an acuteness of judgement or understanding" (Random 377). However, many times discernment is based more on intuitive feelings given by the Holy Spirit rather than on facts and reasoning. Therefore, discernment is not a mathematical equation leading to success because the facts often contradict a discerned answer.

Not long ago, I read a business article about how CEOs in *Fortune 500* companies made their decisions. After all these *Fortune 500* CEOs were given the facts, clearly 40% of them made decisions based on instinct contrary to the facts. In short, the Holy Spirit was giving those business CEOs a "gut feeling" <u>direction</u> about what to do. Thus, decision-making can be taught in business schools, but it can also be sensed through the Holy Spirit. This is the same message that the Holy Spirit gives to a writer. There are writing rules and conventions to follow but there are also creative <u>revelations</u> from the Spirit. For instance, when Ray Bradbury wrote his classic Science Fiction novel *Fahrenheit 451*, Bradbury knew logically that Fahrenheit 451 was the temperature at which paper burned. It's a great fact-based and logical title, given the fact that the novel is about burning books." The autoignition temperature or kindling point of a substance is the lowest temperature in which it spontaneously ignites" (Wikipedia). Yet, while the title is factually accurate about the temperature at which paper burns, the opening scene is not logical; instead, it is highly creative because it follows the Holy Spirit's <u>directive</u>. In *Fahrenheit 451*, the opening scene is a fire truck racing with its sirens blaring on its way to put out a fire. In the reader's mind, a firetruck racing to put out a fire is logical. However, after arriving at a house, the reader is shocked to see that the firehoses spew fire instead of dispensing water. Such inverse cleverness of thought doesn't come from rationale thinking; it comes from the <u>revelation</u> given to the author by the Holy Spirit. Later in the novel, the illogic of the opening scene with firehouses spewing fire instead of water is made logical by the science fiction novel's plot. The government firetrucks are spewing fire instead of water because the government has banned all books, and it is on a campaign to burn them, thereby making the illogic of the opening fire truck scene into something more logical. Of course, fire hoses shouldn't be shooting fire instead of water, that is, unless the <u>creativity</u> supplied to Bradbury by the Holy Spirit makes the reader believe it can happen (Bradbury). This is the difficulty in writing science fiction – making the implausible seem plausible, and this gap can only be filled by the Holy Spirit's gift of <u>revelation</u>. In short, democracy demands the protection of all books from the false prophets of government and that the knowledge found in books should be preserved for all time. Bradbury once said, "I owe all my writing to God" because he knew who supplied him with his ingenious science fiction ideas. "For as many as are led by the Spirit of God, they are the sons of God" (Romans 8:14)

    Therefore, the <u>creativity</u> supplied by the Holy Spirit can't be taught; instead, it can only be <u>envisioned</u> and <u>felt</u> in the heart of the writer by the intuitive feeling supplied by the Holy Spirit. The <u>discernment</u> supplied to the writer by the Holy Spirit requires a storyteller to be trustworthy. The Holy Spirit makes it possible for the writer to tell the <u>truth</u> and for the reader to experience it because their writing is divinely inspired. Therefore, the Holy Spirit is always nudging the writer forward both in writing and in life. "Even the Spirit of truth: whom the world cannot receive, because it seeth him not, neither knoweth him: but ye know him; for he dwelleth with you, and shall be in you" (John 14:17).

Every writer has a Holy Spirit where the <u>creative impulse</u> is grown. The Holy Spirit is like an invisible o-zone layer protecting God's love found in a writer's heart. It is a love put in a writer's heart by Jesus. In fact, Jesus said, "If man love me, he will keep my words: and my Father will love him, and we will come unto him, and make our abode with him" (John14:23). Therefore, God, Jesus, and the Holy Spirit live in all writers, and they provide the supernatural <u>creative impetus</u> and <u>discernment</u> for a writer's work, although many writers may not acknowledge it. Some writers cannot discern the Holy Spirit within them because Satan has hardened their heart. "Wherefore (as the Holy Ghost saith), Today if ye will hear his voice, harden not your hearts" (Hebrews 3:7-8). Writers create essential <u>truths</u> with their words only when the Holy Spirit provides them. "When we tell you this, we do not use words of human wisdom. We speak words given to us by the Spirit, using the Spirit's words to explain spiritual truths" (1 Corinthians 2:13). It is God as the Holy Spirit in them telling them the truth." God is a Spirit: and they that worship him must worship him in spirit and in truth" (John 4:24). Jesus sent the Holy Spirit to <u>comfort</u> us in a world temporarily controlled by Satan. To know what God expects of us as writers, we must live in our Spiritual selves. "For we ... worship God in the spirit, and rejoice in Christ Jesus, and have no confidence in the flesh" (Philippians 3:3).

When the Holy Spirit's help is not called upon by a writer, the writing often remains flat and uninspiring. "When any one hearth the word of the kingdom, and understandeth it not, then cometh the wicked one, and catcheth away that which was sown in his heart" (Matthew 13:19). If writing is a spiritual act guided by supernatural forces, wouldn't it be helpful to access those spiritual powers that can reconcile human writing <u>aspirations</u> with supernatural writing ability? In short, only God can help a writer to improve by aligning their writing aspirations with their life's aspirations. How? By a writer praying to Jesus for help through the Holy Spirit. Prayer is a highly sacred and individual act. By reaching out with prayer to God, a writer is **acknowledging that God exists**, and this is the first step in reconciling with Jesus through the Holy Spirit. But prayer needs to be sincere, and not done for selfish reasons. "And when thou prayest, thou shalt not be as the hypocrites are: for they love to pray standing in the synagogues and in the corners of the streets, that they may be seen of men. Verily, I say unto you. They have their reward" (Matthew 6:5). Therefore, insincere prayers will only incite the wrath of God. So, once you begin to pray, do it from the sincerity of the heart. All goals in life need Jesus through the Holy Spirit to succeed. When writers refuse to acknowledge God, Jesus, and the Holy Spirit's contributions to their work, they neglect responding to the calling of the spiritual trust between them and God. Sadly, writers often arrogantly believe that they write solely from their physical self, which is like accepting living in a rough draft life. While ignoring the Holy Spirit within them, some writers have still attempted to produce words of spiritual truth. This can't be done without allowing the Holy Spirit to participate (e.g., *Walden Pond*). Otherwise, it won't happen because flesh can only talk to the flesh. And Spirit can only to the Spirit! If you chose to write from the perspective of the flesh, you are confined to the thoughts of the flesh. And many writers errantly do it because of their indifference to their own holy being. By ignoring their own spiritual self, some writers neglect God -- the most powerful force in the universe, and instead turn to muses (e.g., alcohol and drugs) to create. Through all things fleshy, they seek spiritual manna for their writing without praying to God through the Holy Spirit to supply it. Unfortunately, for most writers who travel this fleshy path, instead of becoming spiritually enlightened by their muses, they become physically addicted to them. Unfortunately, their bad choices create the darkness causing their own despair. By contrast, the Holy Spirit offers a writer the <u>hope</u> of God's goodness for both a better life and a better writing future because the Holy Spirit's power is not bound to the earth.

Questions

1. Why isn't a rough draft perfect?
2. Who inspires you to make it better?
3. How does a writer produce a meaningful theme?
4. What do most enduring meaningful themes have in common?

Essay 11 The Holy Spirit in the Revision Stage

A final draft of writing is accomplished by a writer polishing the rough draft during the rewriting stage. In this phase the writer becomes a copyeditor to improve their rough draft. In the book publishing industry, copyediting usually involves three types of manuscript development. Copyediting can be light, medium, or heavy. A *light copyedit*, often called a line edit, is merely making small corrections like in grammar, spelling, and mechanics. In short, the writer can write, but they need another set of eyes to review their work. A *medium edit* requires a heavier hand than a light copyedit because a line edit won't alone correct the manuscript's problems. In a medium edit, the copyeditor asks questions about missing content by making notes in the page's margin like supplying examples for further evidence. In short, there are larger missing pieces in a medium edit, but the publisher is still convinced that the content after copyediting will be viable. In a *heavy edit*, a publisher has taken a leap of faith by the Holy Spirit that the manuscript can be fixed editorially. Usually, in heavy edit manuscripts, the author is a leading authority in an academic discipline and has innovative thoughts but is unable to write about them. Heavy editing requires substantial work in reshaping large portions of the manuscript to make it ready for publication. In a heavy edit, a large error is called a *global error* because it impacts the overall value of the manuscript. For example, a missing and necessary chapter qualifies as a global error. The smaller errors are called *local errors* because they only impact the content immediately surrounding the error, although many local errors can add certainly add up to a global error status. This occurs when all the small errors interfere with the writer's ability to communicate with the reader. The decision to classify manuscript as a light, medium, or heavy edit is probably a left-brain and logical activity, although while editing a manuscript the intuitive voice of the

Holy Spirit often <u>guides</u> the copyeditor. The influence of the Holy Spirit in the editorial process can be seen by the advice in the marginal notes that a copyeditor makes to an author. These marginal notes of advice are often subjective guidance and creative suggestions prompted by the Holy Spirit that go beyond the logic of mechanics and grammar. Doing a straightforward light edit (i.e., line edit) is probably a left brained and logical skill. However, when a copyeditor suggests making substantive and creative changes to a manuscript, the copyeditor is probably relying on the creative intuition of the Holy Spirit through the right brain. While the Holy Spirit is involved in helping both the left and right brained dominate writers, it is a fact that right brained people are often predisposed to religion and spiritual pursuits. In turn, one of the Holy Spirit's gifts is <u>sanctification</u>, that is, changing us to be more like Jesus. I believe that writing can do that by listening to the Holy Spirit's advice. "Sanctify them through thy truth: thy word is truth" (John 17:17).

Questions

1. Name three types of copyediting?
2. Why is being able to copyedit your own work valuable?
3. Why do many writers prefer to write than to edit?
4. Why is knowing brain hemisphere dominance helpful when you edit?

CHAPTER 2 WRITERS NEED THE HOLY SPIRIT'S PROTECTION

Essay 12 Satan Endorses a Writer's Destructive Lifestyle

Until Christ returns in triumph, Satan is in temporary control of the earth's economic, social, and political systems. Therefore, writers can always assume that evil is close by. Writing is a reclusive behavior, and sometimes being a writer can be very lonely because writers can get locked inside their own mind. By their nature, writers are complicated, often socially awkward, and many times sensitive and insecure people. Because they often have trouble interacting with the real world, they create their own writing worlds to compensate. Yet, some writers can't distinguish between fact and fiction when they accept that all writers have excessive and destructive lifestyles. Some writers who subscribe to a destructive lifestyle often never get anything published. Frankly, if writers drank as much wine or scotch as the media claimed, they would be too drunk to sit in a chair and write. Granted, some writers were (and are) raging alcoholics, but some doubts remain about the merits of drinking and writing. Therefore, writers, especially young ones, should understand that a publicity image of portraying an over-the-top "writers' lifestyle" and living it are two very different things. Most of the writers that I know are driven by the intoxicating nature of their work supplied to them by the Holy Spirit rather than by living from one alcoholic stupor to the next. After all, Satan doesn't care about your writing; he only wants to take your soul to hell. This is his only mission, and because he controls the earth's economic, political, and social systems until Christ's return, Satan likes to popularize through the media that a writer's life is decadent and romantic. Yet, a writer's reality is far from glamorous. There's nothing glamourous about waking up at 5 am, sitting in your pajamas, sipping a cold cup of coffee, and staring at a blank page. And there's nothing glamourous about working a job full-time on a night shift because you write better in the morning.

Furthermore, drinking a bottle of Scotch Whiskey every day is not enlightening; it is suicidal. Satan knows that writers are vulnerable people because of the anxiety associated with finding the next word. He also knows that writers must chase words through their minds to find them deep inside themselves. And that someplace deep inside of them is their soul where the Holy Spirit resides. Therefore, Satan doesn't want writers thinking, communicating, or collaborating with their Holy Spirit. He wants just the opposite; that's why he encourages sinful behavior that keeps them from writing. Satan doesn't give writers any words to write; God does! Satan's job is to prevent writers from finding any words to write by creating anxiety. This anxiety, in turn, often leads to fear. And when someone is fearful about losing something that they love (i.e., writing), then they will do almost anything to keep it. Thus, Satan tries to take the higher spiritual ground away from a writer by interfering with words and suggesting sinful options. All people are psychologically hotwired for fight or flight. Those writers who can stand their ground and pray for the Holy Spirit's <u>strength</u> to resist Satan's temptations are those writers who understand the basics about life and about successful writing. Having both a good life and being a good writer doesn't happen by accident; it happens because of the intervention of the Holy Spirit through Jesus, because of hard work, and because of prayer.

Throughout history millions of writers have taken a short cut to death because of Satan's influences on their lifestyle choices. Look at the following short list of famous writers who have died young because of alcohol or drug addiction: F. Scott Fitzgerald (age 44), Jack Kerouac (age 47), Edger Allan Poe (age 40), Dylan Thomas (age 39), Truman Capote (60), Ernest Hemingway (62), and James Joyce (58), etc. It seems that being a creative person demands more than what any earthly thing can deliver. Perhaps this is why Mark Twain, Emily Dickinson, Henry David Thoreau, Ralph Waldo Emerson, Saul Bellow, Robert Frost, and James Michener didn't drink alcohol. Satan wants to impede all writers' attempts at writing because the creative gift of writing was given to them by God, and Satan wants to destroy that uniqueness. Satan likes to promote the false notion that all writers are self-destructive. However, most writers are not self-destruction; they're hard working. As mentioned, the media – which is controlled by Satan – likes to spread the myth that the sensitivity of creative people makes them vulnerable to being self-destructive. This may be somewhat true, but the media likes to promote this falsehood because it makes for good copy and attracts an audience that sells more books. This kind of media disinformation creates a barrier between the writer and God, who is the actual author of everything. Therefore, the Holy Spirit can provide <u>strength</u> and <u>guidance</u> away from the destructive forces promoted by Satan.

Questions

1. In general, is a writer's lifestyle glamorous?
2. Why do some media outlets like to promote an excessive writer lifestyle?
3. Do you have to drink alcohol to write?
4. What makes a writer susceptible to drinking?

Essay 13 Satan's Intrusions on a Writer

Ephesians 6:10-12 states that we must be aware of the influence of Satan in the world and plan our personal strategy against him, and this is especially true for a writer. "Finally, my brethren, be strong in the Lord, and in the power of his might. Put on the whole armour of God, that ye may be able to stand against the wiles of the devil" (Ephesians 610-11). So, the Holy Spirit provided by God offers writers the <u>strength</u> to overcome the destructive temptations of Satan. If you believe that everything that goes wrong involves Satan's hand, you would be correct. God cannot do evil only Satan can. Satan's only goal in a writer's life is to provide distractions that impede on a writer's concentration. Satan doesn't care whether you finish your novel. He cares about providing frustration so that you don't. In fact, here is a short list of Satan's interferences to stifle your writing progress: Broken pencils, pens that run out of ink, computer glitches, doorbell rings, snail mail royalty checks, printer cartridges that run out, power failures, missing notes, misplaced mouse, missing power cord, out of computer storage space, robotic cell phone calls, out of printing paper, out of legal pads, and writer's block, etc. Therefore, Satan is both an enemy to writing and to life. Satan doesn't want you to live a long life; he wants a writer to live a short one. If a writer has writer's block, it is most certainly caused by Satan. It is a fact that Satan cannot tell the truth; his evil nature won't allow it, so Satan is the enemy of everyone and everything. He doesn't supply a writer with words; God does through the Holy Spirit. Do you honestly believe that Satan wants you to finish a novel where good triumphs over evil? I think not!

Therefore, a writer must involve the Holy Spirit to do their best writing by <u>protecting</u> themselves against Satan. Praying to Jesus and to the Holy Spirit for <u>protection</u> and <u>joy</u> while writing is extremely important. A war between God and Satan is being waged for your soul, and a writer must not succumb to Satan's destructive urges, either in writing or in life. If you're half-way through writing a novel and can't finish it, blame Satan for the distractions because God is incapable of doing evil. And don't blame yourself either for your lack of progress.; you're doing your best to write forward, but things just aren't going your way. In circumstances like these, where Satan is stringing out your patience and your writing, a writer needs the spiritual <u>protection</u> of the Holy Spirit. On the page, Satan interrupts and disrupts a writer's progress. Off the page, Satan interrupts and disrupts a writer's life to prevent progress by sowing seeds of doubt and despair in a writer's mind. All writers have experienced Satan's presence when he spreads self-doubt in them about their ability to write. Yet, I believe that a computer glitch that deletes 20 manuscript pages is not just a computer glitch; it is Satan stealing the writer's time, work, and patience. Hence, the inability to produce noteworthy writing is not a physical problem but a spiritual one. Without the Holy Spirit's <u>power</u> to combat Satan, a writer is defenseless, both in life and in writing.

Writers Take Note: Many years ago, I attended a seminar in Boston on computer functionality. In the question-and-answer period, the audience asked questions to a panel of computer experts. One person in the audience asked why he could perform a computer function successfully 100 times and then on the 101 try it failed? The computer expert answered, "because it does." In other words, something other worldly and non-technical makes things fail that can't be explained, and that something else is Satan.

Questions

1. Who interferes with a writer's progress?
2. Why does he interfere?
3. Can every writer's setback be explained in rational terms?
4. Can you remember a writing setback that can't be explained?

ESSAY 14 Satan's Economic Influence on Writers

Statistically, only 4% of writers make a living solely from their writing. This means that 96% of writers living in Satan's control of the world are struggling to make financial ends meet by working other jobs. It's true that a job provides both the writer and nonwriter with money. However, working another job for a serious writer is different than for a nonwriter because the writer already has the full-time job of writing. The personal histories of successful writers demonstrate this two-job work patten. Sinclair Lewis worked full time for an insurance company and wrote his Nobel Prize winning novel *Main Street* on the kitchen counter during his lunch breaks. Kurt Vonnegut was a staff writer for General Electric in 1950 and quit to work on writing his first novel *Play Piano* about the insanity of corporate America. In fact, my favorite scene in *Player Piano* involves an escapee of a corporate retreat encountering a farmer with a pitchfork shoveling manure. The farmer offers up his definitions for higher education degrees. To paraphrase, the farmer asks the corporate escapee, "Do you know what B.S. stands for? Well, MS is more of the same, and Ph.D. stands for piled higher and deeper" (Vonnegut, *Player*).

A writer's primary job is to inform a readership by writing quotable responses to complicated social issues, and it takes time and the involvement of the Holy Spirit to formulate them. For instance, the verbosity found in higher education professors could not be made clearer than with the basic story about a farmer piling manure. Such straightforward analogies to explain complicated problems are not easily written because they require the association of two dissimilar things being similar so that a reader can make the connection. To make this association between the attributes of dissimilar things requires the <u>creative prompting</u> of the Holy Spirit. Seeing patterns in dissimilar objects to make them similar is not something logical; it is something illogical and intuitive. In

JD Salinger's *Catcher in the Rye*, the main character is a 15-year-old kid named Holden Caulfield who hides out in a seedy hotel in New York for two weeks after being expelled from a prep school just before Christmas. He can't go home from school early to the suburbs because then his parents will find out that he has been expelled from yet another prep school. On his third night at the hotel, Holden goes down to the hotel bar, the Lavender Room, where he dances separately with three 30-year-old women who were on vacation from Seattle. To compare two of the women's dancing abilities, Holden says, "Lavern wasn't too bad a dancer, but the other one, old Marty...was like dragging the Statue of Liberty around the floor" (Chapter 10). So, based on the physical attributes of the Statue of Liberty applied to Marty's dancing ability, what can we deduce? The Statue of Liberty is constructed of inflexible steel. The Statue of Liberty is very tall. The Statue of Liberty is also very big. The Statue of Liberty is very heavy. So, Marty, the bad dancer, was inflexible, large, tall, and heavy. In short, the Statue of Liberty hasn't moved in decades and neither has Marty (Salinger).

There are 2,080 hours in an average full-time job each year. This calculation is based on 40-hour work week and two weeks of annual vacation. So, any writer can calculate if their writing schedule constitutes a full or part-time job as related to how many hours they spend writing annually. The point is that becoming a writer takes thousands of hours -- or the equivalent of a full-time job -- without any guarantees of success. A writer might never be published, find a readership, or even finish their manuscript. Therefore, the economic risk of spending an enormous amount the time without reward or recognition is high. So, why do people still become writers? Well, they are called by God and <u>instructed</u> by the Holy Spirit to their specific vocation to become writers. In fact, the Holy Spirit guides people to their <u>specific vocation</u>. "We have received not the spirit of the world, but the Spirit which is from God, that we might understand the gifts bestowed on us by God. And we impart this in words not taught by human wisdom but taught by the Spirit" (1 Corinthians 2:12-13). If you really believe that you have been called by God to be a writer, then you should be praying to Jesus for guidance through the Holy Spirit. All writing is God-inspired! "This is the secret: Christ lives in you" (Colossians 1:27).

Because the Holy Spirit was sent by God through Jesus to help a writer, the Holy Spirit can be trusted because God cannot lie. "… it was impossible for God to lie…" (Hebrews 6:18). The Holy Spirit as the sacred messenger from Jesus <u>encourages</u> and <u>inspires</u> the writer because the Holy Spirit cannot do evil, but only good. Therefore, the Holy Spirit's suggestions to a writer are infallibly good because God is infallibly good. In short, a writer can <u>trust</u> the words given to them by the Holy Spirit because the Holy Spirit's words are divinely created. If the Holy Spirit gives a writer the words of <u>truth</u>, why wouldn't a writer accept them? Why wouldn't writers pray to Jesus and the Holy Spirit for <u>help</u> and <u>direction</u>? As a writer, your life with Jesus in it will be more joyful and satisfying. "If so be that ye have heard him, and have been <u>taught</u> by him, as the truth is in Jesus" (Ephesians 4:21).

However, deleting the sin in life isn't as easy as deleting a typo on a manuscript because it is a spiritual adjustment not a physical one. It might take a long time of <u>self-determination</u> supplied by the Holy Spirit to edit sin out of your life so that it becomes more God-centered. "And be not drunk with wine where is excess; but be filled with the Spirit" (Ephesians 5:18). By praying to Jesus for help, by reading the Bible for knowledge, and by listening to the Holy Spirit for guidance, a writer can let God <u>sanctify</u> their life through repentance that leads to a <u>spiritual rebirth</u>. "That which is born of the flesh is flesh; and that which is born of the Spirit is spirit" (John 3:6). However, a writer needs to first embrace the economies of the Holy Spirit's presence in them to strengthen the soul against Satan's influence. The Bible advises the reader to, "Take the helmet of salvation, and the sword of the Spirit, which is the word of God" (Ephesians 6:17). Therefore, God's written Word becomes the spiritual weapon of choice against Satan. This demonstrates the supernatural power of words given by God! Therefore, to truly enjoy the writing experience as a second job, a writer must read the words of the Bible and pray to Jesus for help to be renewed in the Spirit. "...I say unto thee, Except a man be born of water and of the Spirit, he cannot enter into the Kingdom of God" (John 3:5). God's Word in the Bible reveals to a writer how to use the gift of writing given to them by spiritually aligning life with the writing experience. The Holy Spirit <u>gives life</u> to a writer's voice by searching their heart. "Ye are our epistle written in our hearts, known and read of all men...written not with ink, but with the Spirit of the living God; not in tables of stone, but in fleshy tables of the heart" (2 Corinthians 3:2-3).

Questions

1. Can you recall a time when a creative element suddenly appeared without warning?
2. Where did that creative element come from?
3. How did it make you feel as a writer when it arrived?
4. How many hours a year are devoted to writing?

Essay 15 Satan's Use of Fear on a Writer

If everyone could be a prophet and could successfully predict the future, then there wouldn't be any need for fear. Fear derives from an unknown future. For instance, ultimately the fear of death stems from not knowing the Lord Jesus Christ as your personal savior. In particular, fear swarms around a serious writer every day. There is the fear of not being able to write. There is the fear of not being able to write well. There is the fear of not being read. There is the fear of not being good enough. There is the fear of not being published. There is the fear of not having anything meaningful to say, etc. Because writers cannot predict their writing future, they constantly write in a fearful state. To compensate, they either stop writing entirely because it's too frightening, or they work harder. Both responses are nonstarters based on Satan's use of fear. For those writers who suffer a fatal heart attack because they're working too hard to earn something for a "rainy day," their rainy-day expectations just became a deadly season of drought. Every day, Satan wants writers to believe that some future unknown will harm them and that a dark-cloud event hangs over them all the time. If Satan can make a writer fearful about the future of their writing, then he has interjected himself into their work by living in their mind. For example, if while writing a novel, the writer fears that it won't be accepted for publication, then Satan has projected himself into a writer's mind to disconnect him/her from their writing efforts and from their Holy Spirit's <u>comfort</u> and <u>support</u>. On Satan's part, it is pure and simple negative exploitation against a writer's efforts to write. When writers are fearful about their writing's future, they cannot write at their best in the present. If writers search for words with a fear in their heart, then they will eventually succumb to that fear and become impatient and vulnerable to making bad decisions.

For example, Satan knows how to dangle bad literary opportunities in front of discouraged writers at just the right moment, and he takes advantage of a writer's compromised thinking by presenting bad opportunities to them when the writer is the most vulnerable. In the literary world, Satan likes to encourage a writer's impatience because more impatience breeds bad decisions. For example, If the Holy Spirit intuitively tells a writer to be reluctant and hesitant to pursue a literary opportunity, then it is probably a bad one to pursue because the Holy Spirit is <u>guiding</u> their writing to a more promising circumstance. Again, not all literary opportunities for writers are good ones; some are contrived by Satan to sidetrack and discourage a writer. At first glance, many literary opportunities are seemingly in a writer's best interest, yet they turn out to be evil investments for a promising writer's career. Just ask some Nashville songwriters who signed a contract with a shady – yet very convincing -- publishing company that grifted the copyright to their songs. Therefore, relying on the Holy Spirit for <u>direction</u> and <u>guidance</u> in the business of a writing career is very important. One solution for a writer to avoid the pitfalls of the devious plans of Satan is to pray to the Holy Spirit for insight and guidance as to whether the opportunity is coming from the devil or from God. Only praying to Jesus and the Holy Spirit can give you the correct answer.

However, what if writers were no longer fearful about their writing future. What might happen to them if they developed a secure and soulful relationship with Jesus for their writing life through the Holy Spirit? What would Satan do then? The answer to that question is that Satan would flee or at least diminish his evil efforts to destruct their writing career because of the push-back provided by God in favor of a writer's efforts. If a writer prays to God, Jesus, and the Holy Spirit to fight Satan's efforts to derail the success of their writing, then the evil one will certainly have less influence over their life, as well as over their writing. The greater the distance that Jesus through the Holy Spirit can put between a writer and Satan, the better off the writer and the writer's work becomes.

Satan makes writers fearful about the future because he wants to increase his control over them by increasing their stress and anxiety. By doing so, he creates an uncertain mental landscape in a writer's mind that often leads to evil behavior. When writers feel that their future creative efforts are threatened, most will do anything to make their uncertain future more secure. However, when a writer chooses to dance with the devil in the secular world, the music will someday stop. Just ask the Mississippi Delta blues artist, Robert Johnson. Supposedly, Robert Johnson met the devil at a crossroads one night on the outskirts of town and sold his soul to the devil to become a better guitarist. As legend reports it, John returned to town a little while later after his bargain with the devil with superb guitar skills. Later in his life, he was shot and killed by a husband while exiting a married woman's house after sleeping with her. At some level, the myth of Robert Johnson's bargain with the devil eventually influenced the notion that living fast and dying young was somehow a good thing for musicians and that sex and drugs were synonymous with rock music. We won't examine the satanic influence on music right now; perhaps it's a theme for a future book. However, for now, writers need to be aware of Satan's presence near them that could prevent them from pursuing the dream of using their writing talent for good purposes. Perhaps some satanic song lyrics are written to alert us to the nearby presence of Satan. In this scenario, the positive effect of knowing that he is around us outweighs his intention to corrupt us because it alerts us to befriend the Holy Spirit for <u>protection</u>. Therefore, the equation for a writer to live a peaceful and fruitful writing life away from Satan is simple. When you become fearful, pray! Pray to Jesus, pray to the

Holy Spirit, and pray to Father God for <u>strength and direction</u>. The spiritual strength found in prayer and in reading the Bible can fuel a writer's supernatural strength to fight evil and to quell their fears and direct them away from Satan.

Questions

1. Why are writers fearful?
2. Who makes a writer fearful?
3. How does fear impact a writer's productivity?
4. Why does the writer need the Holy Spirit for protection?

CHAPTER 3 MAKING A CONNECTION WITH THE HOLY SPIRIT

Essay 16 Understanding the Holy Spirit

For a writer to connect with the Holy Spirit, they must first understand some basic principles about the divine characteristics of the Holy Spirit. The following characteristics were derived from an article titled *24 Must Know Characteristics of the Holy Spirit* (Wisnewski). Because the Holy Spirit is called God or the Spirit of God and because he is considered God and treated equally to God, the Holy Spirit is often referred to with the pronoun He. The Holy Spirit is also eternal, self-existent, omnipresent, and omniscient. He was involved in creation, enabled the writing of the Bible, helps us to recognize the glory of God, and enables us to call upon Jesus as Lord. In short, the Holy Spirit is part of the Holy Trinity as God.

Besides these divine characteristics, the Holy Spirit also has human characteristics, which are referred to in the Bible. The Holy Spirit is referred to as a **person** (John 6:63, 14:36, Roman 8:11, 16, 26; 1 John 5:6). The Holy Spirit **speaks** (Acts 1:16, 8:29,10:19, 11:12; 1 Timothy 4:1, Hebrews 3:7-8, Revelation 2:27, 14:13, 22:17). The Holy Spirit **can be grieved** (Ephesians 4:30, Isaiah 63:10). The Holy Spirit **loves** (Romans 15:30). The Holy Spirit has a **mind** (Romans 8:27). The Holy Spirit has **intelligence** (1 Corinthians 2:10-11). The Holy Spirit **can be tested** (Acts 5:9). The Holy Spirit can be **resisted** (Acts 7:5). And the Holy Spirit has **a will** (1 Corinthians 2:11, 12:7-11).

Furthermore, according to *moodybible.org*, "The Holy Spirit controls the believer who yields to God and submits himself to God's Word" (Romans 12:1,2; Ephesians 5:18; Colossians 3:16). "When these conditions are met, the believer lives in the power of the Spirit and produces the fruit of the Spirit"

(Galatians 5:16,22,23). "The Holy Spirit indwells in the believer permanently" (1 Corinthians 6:19,20). "While the child of God may sin and grieve the Spirit, the Spirit will never leave the true believer" (Ephesians 4:30) (Moody Bible Institute).

Writers who know that the Holy Spirit is the supernatural originator of their work also have accepted their own holiness and the holiness of their work through Jesus Christ. "Examine yourselves, whether ye be in the faith; prove your own selves. Know ye not your own selves, how that Jesus Christ is in you...?" (2 Corinthians 135). Coming to know Christ has freed many writers from the distractions of Satan's sinful world. "From henceforth let no man trouble me: for I bear in my body the marks of the Lord Jesus" (Galatians 6:17). When Jesus said, "that He has overcome the world" He meant that he had conquered death not only for Himself by His resurrection from death to life, but also for your own resurrection from physical life to spiritual life as well. "These things I have spoken unto you that in me ye might have peace. In the world ye shall have tribulation: but be of good cheer; I have overcome the world" (John 16:33). Therefore, writers should pray for God to anoint their writing. When writers know and feel that Jesus has imparted his gift of salvation on them, they become liberated from their previous fears, as well as freed from the captivity of living in Satan's physical world. In short, a writer whose writing and life live in the Spirit instead of the flesh writes and lives from a divine place. "Those who respond to this conviction and place their faith in Jesus Christ receive eternal life and a new nature" (John 3:3-7; Titus 3:5) (Moody Bible Institute].

The Holy Spirit's influence makes a huge difference on how a writer perceives life, <u>love</u>, and writing. "That he would grant you, according to the riches of his glory, to be strengthened with might by his Spirit in the inner man; That Christ may dwell in your hearts by faith; that ye, being rooted and grounded in love, May be able to comprehend with all saints what is the breadth, and length, and depth, and height; And to know the love of Christ, which passeth knowledge, that ye might be filled with the fulness of God" (Ephesians 3:17-19). Once writers know that they have been granted salvation by Jesus, they understand that life on earth is an individual fight between God and Satan for the possession of their soul. It is a spiritual battle between the influences of good vs evil on and in them, and when their life's thoughts and behavior change for the better, their writing often changes for the better too because they're now under the spiritual protection of Jesus and they're fulfilling their mission as a writer for God.

The great commissions (i.e., responsibility) of every saved Christian is to help other people to receive the salvation message from Jesus. Therefore, by taking the Word of the Lord through their writing to readers, writers become the spiritual connection for helping others to come to Jesus by fulfilling God's writing purpose for them. Every time in writing where good triumphs over evil, it is the Holy Spirit <u>messaging</u> to readers to make good choices in life in the battle for their own souls. "If we live in the Spirit, let us also walk in the Spirit" (Galatians 5:25). When writers come to Jesus through the Holy Spirit, they no longer live in the physical world but in the spiritual world. A writer might still be in their physical body on earth, but they have also transcended spiritually into heaven with Jesus. In effect, they have transitioned away from living totally in the physical body in Satan's fallen world into living an improved spiritual life under God's grace and authority. When a saved Christian writer dies physically, their Spirit immediately moves on to be with Jesus in heaven. By writers becoming a "saved" Christian, they leave behind not the legacy of death but the legacy of life to family and friends. "Without God's Spirit, people are unable to produce fruitful lives that reflect the desires of God" [The Person and Word of the Holy Spirit]. Therefore, even before leaving the earth, writers can help others by shedding God's illuminating presence into the world through their writing so that readers can understand that life is about living for God through Jesus and the Holy Spirit and avoiding Satan. Writers – like everyone -- can either live in the flesh or they can live in the Spirit. God gives free will to every person to make the choice of how to spend their days on earth. Yet, only by living in the Spirit of God's grace can a writer begin to understand how the power of the Holy Spirit works in their life and in their writing for God's purpose for them on earth.

Therefore, when a writer connects with the Holy Spirit through prayer and reading the Bible, a supernatural transformation takes place within that person. It is not an outward physical transformation; a person doesn't suddenly gain 40 pounds of muscle replacing fat, but it is an inward spiritual transformation that strengthens their resolve to **examine thoughts and behavior to *do good in the world***. For a writer this translates into **bringing love to people** with their writing because they see themselves and the world through the Holy Spirit's eyes. "The Spirit itself beareth witness with our spirit, that we are the Children of God" (Romans 8:16) In addition, the Holy Spirit's supernatural energy becomes more alive and active in that writer, and he/she begins to see life on earth from a spiritual perspective and **become more accepting of others** that also influences their writing. In short, God's grace – through the Holy Spirit -- has altered their perspective on life and granted them awareness about God's writing plan for them. In response, they **use every opportunity to be the best person and writer possible. They pray, they confess their sins, they read the Bible, and they try to see the good in all living things**. Furthermore, they have practiced forgiveness in cases where other people have wronged them. The **power of forgiveness** is never-ending because it releases the writer from the bonds of Satan's arms. Thus, when writers connect with Jesus through their Holy Spirit, Satan's negative influence on writers diminishes. "But where sin abounded, grace did much more abound" (Romans 5:20). Many writers have followed this path to connect with the Holy Spirit to find Jesus' gift of salvation. Some of these Christian writers include CS Lewis, J. R.R. Tolkien, Leo Tolstoy, Willa Cather, Wendell Berry, Flannery O'Conner, and Fyodor Dostoyevsky. For these authors and countless other writers and artists, the Holy Spirit has entered their heart and Jesus' gift of salvation has opened their eyes to their own holiness. "That the God of our Lord Jesus Christ, the Father of glory, may give unto you the spirit of wisdom and revelation in the knowledge of him: The eyes of your understanding being enlightened; that ye may know what is the hope of his calling … "(Ephesians 1:17-18).

Questions

1. Name some divine characteristics of the Holy Spirit?
2. Name some human characteristics of the Holy Spirit?
3. Who is the co-writer for all your work?
4. How does accepting the Holy Spirit change you?

The Frost of Lost Words

Essay 17 A Writer's Spiritual Identity

    A writer's success can be defined in both secular and spiritual terms. In Satan's secular world, success is defined by how much money a writer makes. However, that same writer's success can also be defined in spiritual terms as having achieved a long-awaited first novel by overcoming many of Satan's obstacles. Only God can define a writer's success because He has always had a plan for their writing. For instance, maybe God's plan for your writing through the Holy Spirit was to be read by only one person because God wanted your writing to influence that one person spiritually. Therefore, how, when, and who your writing impacts is also controlled by God. As a writer, you write because God has ordained it and that should be a writer's sole purpose – to write. Why a writer writes is God's area of expertise. And who reads a writer's work is also God prerogative. Therefore, a writer should not labor under the false notions of Satan that how many people read their work or how much money they make defines its value. It doesn't. What matters is that you are performing as a writer as God's will for you. Thus, any delusions of Satan about expecting fame and fortune should be discarded because writing is a sacred act and not a secular one. In its truest sense, writing is an act of purity where one person's love helps to define another person's life in more perfect terms. In short, writing is an act of love because the <u>insight</u> given to a writer by God through Jesus and the Holy Spirit is given back to the reader. In this context, Satan's money and fame definition of success seem crass and out of place, although Satan doesn't make people writers; God does. Therefore, Satan shouldn't be defining success for a writer. Writers should follow their Holy Spirit's advice to elicit the writing that God commands of them and to ignore the advice of evil forces. Sometimes writers need to hit rock bottom in life before they understand that writing is a sacred act of devotion to God. However, when a writer realizes through the Holy Spirit that they are not writing for themselves but for the Holy One, a moment of personal <u>illumination</u> ensues. At this moment, they understand that writing is really caused by the Holy Spirit and Jesus working on their heart. The Holy Spirit's <u>intervention</u> into a writer's heart also causes an artistic epiphany in a writer's life, one that leads their works away from themselves and into God's hands. Because of their new spiritual <u>awareness</u>, a writer can make greater sense of the world and their place in it. Once a writer realizes through the Holy Spirit that they are really working for God, what writing means to them changes because they have become aware of their holy purpose. No longer are they simply physically moving words across the page to be read, but they are moving them across the page by the intent of the Holy Spirit for God's purpose. Eventually, this realization that writing is a sacred mission becomes paramount to them, and writing is no longer defined by Satan's earthy success but by supernatural spiritual inclination. In short, they have stopped relying on themselves for answers in life and writing and they have finally connected with the Holy Spirit's voice. "Blessed are the pure in heart: for they shall see God" (Matthew 5:8).

Unfortunately, many writers never know that writing is a sacred pursuit because they are tone-deaf to the holiness in them and their spiritual identity. Consequently, some writers will remain perpetually disappointed in their work because their novel didn't get published and appear on the *New York Times Best Seller List*. By contrast, writers who accept the Holy Spirit's direction for their writing also accept God's Will for their life. If a writer's books don't sell before the author's death, God might still have a readership for them afterward. In fact, Herman Melville's American classic *Moby Dick* was panned by the critics and not widely read while Melville was alive. In fact, Melville died believing that *Moby Dick* was an abysmal failure. Yet, God had other plans for his book. Writers who live in the Spirit accept God's Will over their own. If one person reads a book and comes to Jesus, then the book is a success. So, like everything else in life, success can be defined in both physical terms and spiritual terms.

Questions

1. Should a writer be working for fame and fortune?
2. Name two ways to define writing success?
3. Who should writers be writing for?
4. Why Herman Melville's Moby Dick important an important example of success?

Essay 18   Using the Secular World for Moral Instruction

Frankly, I don't understand why some people want to ban books from libraries that they deem profane. Those books found on a library shelf have been vetted by peer reviewers and critics to become acceptable library materials, given the author's use of language pertinent to the subject matter. Yet, no such vetting exists for internet filth that is readily available. Today, the internet reminds me of a digital form of Sodom and Gomorrah where anything goes sexually if you can pay for it. But let's keep to the point: I believe that literature including profanity is fine if the language depicts the accuracy of the characters and eventually creates a moral lesson for the reader; therefore, the seemingly inappropriate language needs to be understood within the entire context of what is being proposed morally by the writer. I recently reread *The Catcher In The Rye* by JD Salinger, and I must admit that I grimaced at the vulgar language uttered by the protagonist, a 15-year-old kid named Holden Caulfield. Yet, I knew 15-year-old kids in my neighborhood while growing up who used the same language, and to me Holden Caulfield's language in *The Catcher in the Rye* was necessary to emphasize the uninformed and immature nature of his character. Ultimately, however, at the end of the book, there appears to be a realization of maturity in Holden about how the adult world operates when he wants to save all the children in the world from the pain of falling over the cliff from childhood into adulthood. And at that moment, Holden's off-color language even makes greater sense throughout the novel because the novel was a coming-of-age experience for Holden, complete with all the flaws of adolescence, including the amplification of foul language, which is one of Holden major adolescent flaws. So, I submit that the language in *Catcher in the Rye* is essential in defining the adolescent ignorance of Holden, who finally at the end of the novel begins to understand how the adult world works. Now, whether Holden cleaned up his language after that, who knows? Maybe the book's critics would have been more understanding of Holden's language in *Catcher In The Rye* if in a subsequent book Holden becomes a well-spoken graduate of an Ivy League school.

But let's be clear, a writer's mission on earth is not to profane the Word of God or grieve the Holy Spirit but to instruct readers on moral conduct. Because of his maturation at the end of the novel, Holden's profane language seems to be a passing phase in his life, and most adolescents feel like their lives are being controlled by the adult world, which is a world that they cannot yet understand. A writer has a sacred mission to help readers to better understand human nature in the world. If by using vulgar language spoken unknowingly by an adolescent character is essential to the plot's maturation of a character, then a writer helps readers to better understand the world, and the writer has succeeded in their job to inform and instruct.

James 3 illustrates how improper and evil a "tongue" can be if not controlled. It states simply that many people – like Holden in *The Catcher In the Rye* -- don't think about what they say before they say it, and this causes many problems for the speaker. Holden's life is full of adolescent problems, and his language certainly doesn't help him to solve them. So, Holden's character and his sinful speech seems consistent with the problems caused by language as stated in the Bible. In fact, James 3 states that a runaway mouth is like a runaway horse, and while we seek to control most things – like a bridle controls a horse – we neglect restricting our own words through self-control. "Out of the same mouth proceedeth blessing and cursing. My brethren, these things ought not so to be" (James 3:10). Therefore, someone who does not control what they say is being offensive to God; they try to say things that are both pleasing to people and to God, yet they should only say things that are pleasing to God. So, like most people who speak too much and say too little, they prattle on with vulgarity about nothing important, or worse yet, amplify rumors and gossip with "backbiting" speech. "But shun profane and vain babblings: for they will increase unto more ungodliness" (2 Timothy 2:16). In fact, James 3:15 classifies this type of unflattering speech as evil. "This wisdom descendeth not from above, but is earthly, sensual, devilish" (James 3:15). Accordingly, vulgar language is manmade and not God-inspired, and it diminishes people from their holy state because it grieves the Holy Spirit and because it is provoked by the brutish instincts of human nature and is not of God. James 3 refers to the uncontrollable tongue as evil. It is a lack of self-control that "defileth the whole body, and sitteth on fire the course of nature, and it is set on fire of hell" (James 3:6). Therefore, when someone gossips, utters frequent vulgarities, or lies, they are engaging in beastly behavior unbecoming to God. In short, although the tongue is a small member of the body, speech can create a greater evil disproportionate to the tongue's size. "Even so the tongue is a little member, and boasted great things. Behold how great a matter a little fire kindleth!" (James 3:5).

Therefore, on one hand, a writer has an obligation to instruct morally, to inform readers, and to give readers insight about the world, yet on the other hand a writer has an obligation through the Holy Spirit not to disturb or destroy their relationship with God. Certainly, a person who spouts profanities and gossips without thinking while knowing better falls into this evil category. Some people swear so much that they don't even know they're doing it! Therefore, like all things Christian, exercising <u>thought</u> and <u>discretion</u> though the Holy Spirit before speaking is key to controlling one's tongue. Holden Caulfield's problem in *The Catcher In The Rye* is that he is an adolescent in search of himself in an adult world and doesn't know better, and he tries erroneously to express himself in what he believes to be adult language. And it is true that while some adults can control their eating habits, they are still unable to control their speaking habits.

Many people don't control their vulgarity and gossip because they falsely believe that it empowers them, and in *The Catcher In The Rye* this is Holden Caulfield's adolescent perspective. For example, it doesn't matter to Holden if what is said is true; it is the shock value of the information that gets him attention. However, the shock value of anyone's language and gossip doesn't create power. It demonstrates ignorance. And fortunately for the reader of *The Catcher in The Rye*, the author has Holden in the end display some assemblance of adult maturation when he wants to save his little sister from the pains of growing up. Perhaps a *Volume II of The Catcher In The Rye* where Holden matures into a well-spoken adult would have alleviated the critics response to the language.

Questions

1. Do you feel that literary classics should be banned from the library?
2. What is the difference between the library content and other places?
3. When should a character's language be defined as obscene?
4. Ultimately, what does a writer seek to accomplish in society when writing?

Essay 19 Writing the Unbiased Truth

Every writer needs to understand their spirituality quotient. That is, how much of them is living for God and how much of them is living for themselves in the flesh? Because a writer needs to find their spiritual self to find their personal "completeness" to do their best writing, they must pray for supernatural guidance from the Holy Spirit and Jesus to find it. Ephesians 6:10-12 states this fact by taking us to the appropriate battleground to do battle with the appropriate enemy. "Finally, my brethren, be strong in the Lord, and in the power of his might. Put on the whole armour of God, that ye may be able to stand against the wiles of the devil. For we wrestle not against flesh and blood, but against principalities, against powers, against the rulers of the darkness of this world, against spiritual wickedness in high places." Therefore, when writers compete against other writers on earth for money, status, and power, they are fighting the wrong enemy on the wrong battlefield. The essential battle in life is found inwardly in the soul. I'm sure that God notices those people who function morally in an immoral world. However, if Satan convinces writers that being sinful is in their best interests to win at the writing game, then writers lose a step in the most important walk of life – the battle for their soul.

Because some people are ordained by God to be writers, they are supposed to be those people who uphold moral truth. For instance, writers are obligated by moral principle not to plagiarize and to give credit to all sources found in their work. Writers who fail to give appropriate credit to other writers whose work is in their own are deemed less than credible on earth and less than honorable in heaven. Also, a writer who quotes another person yet takes the quote out of context is also deemed second rate. All writers stand on the moral shoulders of previous writers. For example, when writers begin to research a long magazine article, they soon discover that those writers who have written previous articles about the topic are invaluable to them. Reading books and articles by previous writers increases their own knowledge base. However, if fake and inaccurate information exists in that knowledge base produced by former writers, then the truthful outcome of the present writer becomes unreliable and questionable. Thus, a writer has a <u>moral obligation</u> through the Holy Spirit to research accurately and to write truthfully by giving a full account of those other authors who have contributed to the work. God has not given a writer their talent to be used for spinning lies for Satan; God has given a writer their special talents to make the world a more truthful place. "For what is a man profited, if he shall gain the whole world, and lose his own soul? Or what shall a man give in exchange for his soul?" (Matthew 16:27)

Of course, the internet is still a wild west show for producing untruthfulness because of the inaccuracy of so much writing on it. Driven by the bias of hate, revenge, prejudice, and anger, some writers purposely follow Satan's directions by spewing false information. In fact, the internet has made genuine, truthful writing more difficult to find because of the proliferation of false narratives. This misinformation and disinformation have made the world more prone to evil because falsehood is now being mainstreamed as the truth. For example, when I was a child, television news commentators just objectively read the news to the public from a teleprompter. The commentators weren't the news; they were just the reporters of it. In fact, back in the day, a slight voice inflection that displayed a reporter's biased opinion could get a newscaster fired. I remember Walter Cronkite being criticized for showing his emotion on-air while reporting live about the assassination of President John F. Kennedy just moments after it had occurred. But today, news programs invite other news commentators onto their programs to voice their opinions on topics, as if they were experts. Today, many news writers and commentators have become celebrities – not because of what they know but because of how their personalities deliver the news to their viewing audience for program ratings. Therefore, celebrity and popularity have now become more important than telling or writing the informed and complete truth in an unbiased way. Remember: Satan is incapable of telling the truth, so everything that he controls is a lie. So why would Satan rig a news system to tell the truth when he doesn't even know it himself? He can't and won't. Satan is the largest purveyor of the inversion of truth to have ever existed, and his influence on every earthly resource cannot be underestimated. In fact, everything that Satan has ever suggested to you is a lie because he is the prime mover of false information in the world. A bricklayer can't leave one brick out of a wall and call it right. People who bag your groceries in the store can't leave one item out of the bag and call it right. What makes writers think that they can intentionally leave details out, write half-truths, and call it right? "...whosoever therefore will be a friend of the world is the enemy of God" (James 4:4). Therefore, writers should do some soul searching about writing the unbiased truth by connecting with the Holy Spirit sent by Jesus to inform them. "Submit yourselves therefore to God. Resist the devil, and he will flee from you" (James 4:7).

Questions

1. Why does a writer have a moral obligation?
2. What is the difference between an original work and those that follow?
3. Are celebrities really experts in the field of study?
4. Why does the media ask them for their perspective?

Essay 20 Writing to Draw Closer to God

Today, it seems that saying "thank you" to someone has become a lost art. I am an old school person, my parents taught me right from wrong, and to say, "thank you" to show appreciation, and throughout my life I have complied, although many people today didn't get the memo about being courteous. For example, not long ago I was in Chicago, and I was entering a store on Michigan Ave when I opened and held the door for the person in front of me. Instead of thanking me for opening the door, they retorted, "Does it look like my arms are broken?" Over the years, I've tried to keep complying with the wishes instilled in me by my parents, but frankly, every year it's getting more and more difficult because people don't seem to appreciate manners anymore. In a world that's being dumbed down by Satan to create turmoil, I can see why they don't. This adherence to being unpolite, uncaring, and lacking empathy for others is created by Satan in direct defiance of biblical scripture. Of course, this is Satan's way of perpetuating the disharmony in society. He likes to spread anger, violence, and division in society by influencing intolerance and splintering goodwill. I'm sure that the person at the department store door thought they were defending their right to be autonomous, and I get that. Yet, opening a door for someone is such a simple favor; I wonder if that same person would make the same hurtful comment to me if I had stopped to change a flat tire on their car at midnight on rainy night on a lonely road?

By contrast, the Holy Spirit <u>inspires</u> writers to always be <u>empathic</u> and <u>forgiving</u> towards other people. After all, Jesus *is love* yesterday, today, and tomorrow, and by aspiring to be more Christ-like by monitoring their behavior, writers can become closer to Jesus during their lifetime. Bringing a person (e.g., writer) closer to Jesus to be more like Him is called <u>sanctification</u>, and it is another job of the Holy Spirit. Praying for Jesus' help and accepting His <u>advice</u> through the Holy Spirit in their life brings a writer closer to Jesus and to God. In turn, this will bring a writer closer to the spiritual quality found in their writing. God is the ultimate writer in the universe. He created it all. Therefore, when writers seek His help through prayer and reading the Bible, they are making a powerful one-on-one supernatural connection. I know many writers who pray for help throughout the day because they know that Satan controls the earth's systems and that his evil influence is stronger than their own human will power to resist it. Praying to God, His Son Jesus, and The Holy Spirit gives them the additional <u>strength</u> to fight Satan's evil suggestions that distract them from writing. This holy strength derived from praying to the Holy Trinity throughout the day results in writers making <u>better decisions</u>, feeling more spiritually <u>empowered</u>, and being more <u>at peace</u> with themselves and their writing. In short, writers who pray to God and involve Jesus and the Holy Spirit in their lives often feel God <u>giving</u> back to them in every aspect of their lives, including their writing.

All writing must sustain a certain level of vitality through the words chosen to elicit a personal impact. The words must create a life of their own to gain the reader's interest and keep it. Yet, often what an author writes becomes only noticeable to a reader when an important message is written in an inventive way. Thus, the <u>creative inventiveness</u> found in a writer's style applied to the work by the author is important because it includes the Holy Spirit's participation. Only through the Holy Spirit can a writer understand how words supernaturally given can change the outcome of a work by amplifying its impact. With the Holy Spirit's involvement, a writer can feel the otherness operating in themselves and in what they choose to write. In this state of supernatural cooperation, the writer no longer feels alone but absorbs a sacred light that leads them closer towards writing's perfection. The co-writing of the Holy

Spirit improves them and their work by adding <u>guidance</u> and <u>wisdom</u>.

    Therefore, the physical act of writing is a rote exercise, unless the wisdom of the Holy Spirit is included to add depth. Without the Holy Spirit's <u>wisdom</u>, writing will never reach its full potential. Writing by itself cannot give life to itself; the words must have the Holy Spirit's permission to live. Thus, the subliminal and emotional vitality of a piece of writing is not caused by abstract physical words; it is caused by the sacred intervention of the Holy Spirit's power to infuse holiness. Therefore, writing is a supernatural expressive act that must be journeyed as such by a writer to produce spiritual fruit. For instance, in some works of fiction, the Holy Spirit is so apparent in the author's work that the work itself takes on a spiritual life of its own because of its own spiritual essence. These types of classic works of literature go straight to the heart from start to finish. To me, The *Hobbit* by JRR Tolkien qualifies as a spiritually inspired book because the Holy Spirit's presence as co-writer improves everyone's life who reads it.

    Journeys of the Spirit can go in many directions and travel by many modes of transport, and I believe that writing is a journey to find the Spirit's involvement in a writer's life. In short, the Holy Spirit can transport every writer's soul closer to Jesus by what they search for and what they write about. Being in search of one's spiritual potential through their writing is a very humbling experience, yet it is an honorable journey. It's true that writing can be tedious, but it can also be inspirational and spiritually therapeutic. How can the Holy Spirit's power and wisdom flowing through a writer and the writer's work not make both better? Any writer who can feel the flow of wisdom from the Holy Spirit entering them and their work while they create must also know that they are not alone in that act of creation. They must feel that some supernatural force is being exerted on them that exists beyond themselves. And by humbly submitting to it, they become better people and better writers. This is the ultimate Spiritual experience for a writer because it brings the writer closer to God.

Thus, writing as a supernatural experience can improve both the writer's life and their writing by transporting both perspectives to a higher spiritual space. This spiritualization of a writer occurs when they finally focus their writing on the welfare of others and not solely on the welfare of themselves. Therefore, one important point to becoming a good writer is to let the real adventure begin by allowing the sanctification of yourself to begin. The essential journey of any writer involves the <u>sanctification</u> process of moving them closer to Jesus.

Questions

1. Are writers on a journey of the Spirit?
2. If so, what does the Holy Spirit's influence give the writer?
3. Who gives the writer wisdom?
4. Without the Holy Spirit, can a writer reach their full potential?

Essay 21 The Hidden Spiritual Writer of the Heart

1 Peter 3:4 states, "But let it be the hidden man of the heart, in that which is not corruptible, even the ornament of a meek and quiet spirit, which is in the sight of God great price." The phrase "hidden man" of the heart is curious because it implies that some part of a person (e.g., writer) is hidden from the rest of them. That is, somewhere within a writer lies a person in hiding who they haven't yet discovered. The part of a writer that is hidden from them is the Spirit residing in their heart. Therefore, a writer's spiritual self must be discovered so that the "hidden spiritual writer" can be revealed and become a part of their life. So, if we know the identity of the hidden person (i.e., The Spirit) and where the hidden Spiritual person is hiding (i.e., the heart), then that spiritual person isn't really hidden anymore because we have revealed its identity and its hiding place, although many times we have not accessed it. Our "hidden spiritual person" is the living God in us through the Holy Spirit sent by Jesus to save use from Satan's sins of damnation. The Spirit lives and hides in our heart until Jesus Christ awakens him in us through the Holy Spirit. Therefore, the "hidden person" for writers is their inner, unknown spiritual/writer self, that is, the person and writer that they could become. I believe it's a question of living as a complete or incomplete writer and person. For a writer, living as an incomplete spiritual person means always chasing after their elusive writing potential. Writers who lack the <u>strength</u> and <u>inspiration</u> of the Holy Spirit know that they can write better, but don't know how to do it. A complete writer who is in fellowship with the Holy Spirit knows through Jesus the identity of their hidden-writer-self because the supernatural fellowship completes them. Therefore, because the "hidden person" is both spiritual and incorruptible, accessing the spiritual self makes them a better person. "… in that which is not corruptible." So, somewhere in a writer's heart lives

another incorruptible spiritual-writer self. "Incorruptible" means that their spiritual self is pure and cannot be undefiled by Satan's ways of the world. In other words, a purer and untarnished Spiritual You exists within your writing-self. The spiritualized writer is a more perfect self; therefore, their writing is a more perfect expression of themselves. It's like a long-distance track runner who can never access their second wind to reach their running potential, although they know it is within them. This simile points to the unfinished business in a writer's life and heart. A writer can, indeed, find their second wind in both life and in writing, if they search their heart for the unrealized potential found in their Holy Spirit.

Furthermore, "Let not the hidden man be outrageous in appearance and boastful about deed because he is the hidden spirit of man residing in his heart. But let the man be an ornament (example) of the meek and quiet spirit, where peace resides" (1 Peter 3:4). Writers who truly understand their spiritual selves by connecting with their Holy Spirit as sent to them by Jesus Christ know their "hidden spiritual obligation" and know how to live an appreciative life because they also know that their power to write stems from the supernatural power of God. Therefore, a spiritual self is both concealed – yet revealed by Jesus —and resides in the heart of a "writer-you" as the Holy Spirit, given to you by Jesus to give you <u>guidance and comfort</u> on earth.

However, some writers may never know their genuine writer's voice hidden in their spiritual writer- self because they never discover its hiding place. This is because they have been convinced by Satan not to look for it. "He that is of God hearth God's words: ye therefore hear them not, because ye are not of God" (John 8:47). Therefore, the strongest part of their writing potential – God's will -- remains hidden for them without introduction. This is shameful because God is well-pleased by those people who walk according to their spiritual selves. 1 Peter 3:4 states, "... which is in the sight of God great price." So, God loves people who find, rely upon, and pray to their Holy Spirit to believe in something of great price. Something of "great price" is extremely valuable to the owner. Therefore, for a writer connecting with their spiritual writer- self is priceless because it presents another part of themselves to their writing where more soulful and expressive words reside. This expansion of spiritual awareness from living and writing in the physical body to living and writing in the spiritual body serves the writer well because it illuminates their life's path. This means a greater spiritual connection between their writing and themself and a greater spiritual connection between God in them. Therefore, writing from a holy perspective brings out the best in everyone and everything. Thus, the spiritual-writer-self connects the search for words from the Holy Spirit and Jesus, and this, in turn, provides the love and comfort of Jesus in the writing process and in life.

Questions

1. Who is the hidden person inside yourself?
2. Who put that other person there?
3. For what reason do you have that other person within you?
4. What does it mean to a writer to have the Holy Spirit's blessing?

The Frost of Lost Words

Essay 22 Make Your Holiness the Focus

The scripture found in Philippians 4: 5-7 is good instruction for living a spiritual writing life. "Let your moderation be known unto all men. The Lord is at hand" (Philippians 4:5). Satan's world is about more is better. More money. More cars. More houses. In Satan's world moderation doesn't exist. This is because Satan prefers to keep you busy by continually having you strive for something more; it's his way of keeping you unsatisfied. From Satan's viewpoint, there is never enough of anything, so you need to work harder in the false hope of being satisfied by the possibility of having enough of something someday. Yet, Philippians 4:5 says just the opposite about God's worldview. "Let your moderation be known unto all." The Bible states that moderation and not excess is the key to finding peace and happiness. When you read the Bible for instruction about living life honorably through the Spirit, then you must be prepared to see life through God's eyes instead of through Satan's.

For a writer, living a moderate life unlocks one of the great mysteries to living peacefully and writing better. By choosing not to follow Satan's endless and delusional pursuit of physical things, your writing reboots itself through the Holy Spirit to the priorities of its former <u>promise</u>. A less-is-better mindset in all consumption practices frees a writer's mind and heart to concentrate on writing and spiritual growth. By writers focusing their attention on what is spiritually essential and important to them in life and by deleting the remainder, they now have more time to reflect on their spiritual life and writing. This type of inner spiritual journey to dialogue with yourself about your spirituality usually occurs by the <u>promptings</u> of the Holy Spirit. Remember, Satan doesn't want you to reflect on your spiritual self to write; he wants you to keep moving and doing other things. By taking the time to slow your life down by uncomplicating it by releasing yourself from the time spent to pursue too many things that act as distractions, a writer becomes freed from self-obsession and becomes less self-absorbed with things that Satan provides to interfere with their spiritual self and writing. In turn, freedom is gained by expelling the uselessness of many of Satan's influences, and a writer has more time and becomes more focused on what's important in life. To a writer, it means having more time to devote to writing to become better at it. Living a full life doesn't mean living a complicated one with things that you don't need and with friends who only know greed. Henry David Thoreau's *Walden Pond* is an excellent example of the Holy Spirit empowering someone to live moderately by removing themselves physically from society to examine themselves spiritually. The first paragraph in *Walden Pond* explains Thoreau's intent to remove himself from society to gain a greater spiritual understanding and reawakening. "When I wrote the following pages, or rather the bulk of them, I lived alone, in the woods, a mile from any neighbor, in a house which I had built myself, on the shore of Walden Pond, in Concord Massachusetts, and earned my living by the labor of my hands only. I lived there two years and two months. At present I am a sojourner in civilized life again" (1). In effect, Thoreau lived by "roughing it" in the woods on Walden Pond to become more spiritually acquainted with himself. This, in turn, gave him a better perspective on what's important in life. This is what Thoreau wrote in his journal about acquiring material possessions. "Why should they begin digging their graves as soon as they are born? They have got to live a man's life, pushing all these things before them, and get on as well as they can. How many a poor immortal soul have I met well-nigh crushed and smothered under its load…" (2). To Thoreau, moderation and simplicity seemed to be the key to living a better and more spiritually aware life.

I believe that Thoreau stated the exact length of time (i.e., two years and two months) that he spent on Walden Pond to remind the reader that time is a nonrenewable resource. You can get more money, but you can't get more time. The irony is that God keeps giving us more and more time throughout the centuries by extending our life expectancy in hopes that we will turn towards Him, but we still don't. For example, the life expectancy – that is, how long someone statistically is supposed to live – has been lengthening throughout history. During Jesus' time a poor farmer might live 20 to 40 years, while the life expectancy in the US today is over 80 years. Yet, while God keeps extending the years of a human life, many writers have yet to receive the spiritual memo about why? Furthermore, there is debate about at what age a writer produces their best work. I have read that if a writer hasn't published a critically acclaimed novel by the age of 27 that he/she is a has-been by literary standards. Of course, this is nonsense. Many writers continue writing their best work until the final days of their life. I remember seeing a photograph of former US President Ulysses S. Grant sitting wrapped in a blanket in a chair on his porch still writing his memoir five days before his death. Grant knew that he needed to finish his memoir to give his family financial security after his death. I found the photograph poignant for many reasons. First, its honorable that he knew that his writing would save his family from becoming destitute and he continued to write until his death. Second, because of this realization about his family's economic circumstances, he probably continued to write until his last moments on earth relying on the <u>strength</u> of the Holy Spirit. In the photograph he looked physically frail and gaunt. And third, he's writing his last memoir pages outdoors, a place where in five days freedom awaits the release of his Spirit.

At what age a writer finds their peak writing ability is up to the Holy Spirit. The Holy Spirit develops a writer's <u>ability</u> in supernatural time and not in Eastern Standard Time. Therefore, how fast writers can progress in their God-given vocation depends on the depth of the Holy Spirit's involvement, and peak performance can arrive at any age. The 27-year-old novelist theory is probably a fast-track, secular idea promoted by Satan to develop disappointment in a writer's mind at a young age, and it surely must have been based on secular data about how fast a writer must develop to achieve money and power. In fact, literary agents who want to make the most commission from an artist's creativity prefer younger artists because they can keep them under contract for a longer creative period of time. Some agents make an entire career mostly from promoting the creative efforts of one artist; just ask Col. Parker, the agent for Elvis.

Questions

1. Why is Henry David Thoreau's lifestyle on *Walden Pond* a good example?
2. What does the secular world say about moderation?
3. What does the Bible say about moderation?
4. Can a writer create good writing at any age?

Essay 23 The Motivation of Greed and Success

Previously, I wrote that writers create thoughts through words because God through Jesus and the Holy Spirit have intended for them to be a writer. Even with setbacks, writers continue to write because they must. Being compelled to be a writer can be very frustrating in a world that often doesn't understand art or an artistic personality. People tend to understand only the utility of things, and the most utilized thing on earth is money. It's true that money can buy almost anything. For instance, money can buy convenience, but it cannot buy happiness. True and lasting happiness is supplied by God. However, in Satan's world, happiness is seemingly up for sale because everything is for sale at the right price. Yet, the only thing that money can't purchase is faith. Faith is given by God and cannot be acquired unless God sends it. You can buy religion and all the trappings of the church, and you can enjoy the fellowship of other church members, but genuine faith is sent by God. One of the ways that the Holy Spirit reveals faith to a writer is through their ability to grow as a writer. The Holy Spirit leads everyone to their vocation and instructs them on how to improve, and this includes writers. When I was growing up, my father always told people that I wasn't very mechanically inclined. It's true; I wasn't. But the question remains: Why wasn't I? Why did I become a writer, although I can't fix the brakes on my car? The answer is that vocational skills are given by God through Jesus and the Holy Spirit. In short, your occupation was chosen for you by God before you were born. God gave you the specific intellect to do what He wanted you to do on earth in life. In my case, it was to become a writer and a teacher of it. Then, it is up to me by the guidance of the Holy Spirit to improve and to do it as well as I can. So, both the inclination to be a writer and the innate talent to become a writer were both given to us by God. The Holy Spirit through Jesus guides and directs people on how to become and improve as a writer, but the essence of who you are – a writer –was determined long before your birth. God designed you to be a writer, and then you were born to be one, and then Jesus sent the Holy Spirit to help you to grow to become one. Therefore, supernatural forces were at play at every phase of your existence. They not only created you, but they also gave your specific skills to carry forth on a mission for God. And now, you are a writer, and you will grow as one because the Holy Spirit <u>directs</u>, <u>guides</u>, and <u>comforts</u> all writers, no matter on what writing progress path they travel.

Before you were born, you were already a writer in-the-making in the womb. God, Jesus, and the Holy Spirit knew you as a writer and they still live in you today. They never left you because they wanted to develop you spiritually as both a person, as well as you vocationally as a writer. God didn't give life to you to aspire to be anything else but a writer; it was His vocational calling for you. He gave you a life to become a writer and to write the Words of Truth about His kingdom. By understanding and taking God's direction for you to be a writer, you also understand that God is the author of your life and for your talents; moreover, you also have been <u>prompted</u> by the Holy Spirit through Jesus to reject Satan's relentless pursuit of working harder to buy more things. By living moderately while focusing spiritually, you show others a different path to peace through the <u>instruction</u> of the Holy Spirit. Yet, the problem isn't so much recognizing that writers are often working their selves to death; it is how to step off Satan's fast- moving train of destruction?

Although most writers recognize that their obsession with writing is often creating an unhealthy lifestyle, they are still unwilling – or unable -- to step off Satan's fast-moving cycle of secular interests. It is difficult to change a lifestyle devoted to things and replace it with one devoted to spiritual purpose through writing. And don't forget that until Jesus Christ returns to earth that Satan temporarily controls the earth's economic, social, and political systems; thus, Satan's influence on our earthly lives is massive, and he has ingrained in writers to work hard to compete to climb the literary ladder. In many respects, by neglecting God and their spiritual health, some writers eventually become the economic, social, and political tools of Satan's world of sinful behavior and over consumption. Satan wants all writers to believe that only he knows what's best for them. Yet Satan is the only one who would agree that you should work yourself to death. Your family wouldn't agree with it, nor would your friends or loved ones. Therefore, what makes Satan in such a big hurry for a writer to die by adopting an unhealthy lifestyle? What's in it for him?

Of course, while working hard and compromising your physical health by chasing after literary fame, Satan will tell you that your writing life is great. You have just written and finished a third novel, have two speaking engagements this week, and the medicine to prevent your heart attack is doing wonders. According to the Evil One, his things on earth can provide all writers with everything that they need, including progress towards future happiness. Yet, upon a writer's death after the heart attack that the medicine couldn't prevent and upon a closer scrutiny about how they had lived their hectic life, Satan becomes the big winner. First, when writers work (or drink) themselves to death, ignore their spiritual health, and die young by compromising their physical health, Satan has succeeded in making them think that working themselves to death for literary success is more important than their spiritual well-being. Second, by keeping writers busy throughout their life while working ever harder and harder chasing after literary dreams, he has kept them too occupied to think about God, Jesus, and the Holy Spirit and their more important spiritual self. "Neglect not the gift that is in thee, which was given thee by prophecy..." (1 Timothy 4:14). And then, of course, third, if you die young without the knowledge of your spiritual self through Jesus and the Holy Spirit, Satan gets to dispatch your soul to hell. So, in this hard-working, fast-living scenario, Satan becomes a trifecta winner. And like most things in life when somebody wins then somebody loses. And unfortunately, in this fast-living, hard-drinking scenario, a writer becomes the big loser. If Satan can press a writer's psychological buttons to use their writing for secular aspirations like to compete for money and power, then he can successfully jumpstart your life and its meaning into the realm of alcoholism and drug addiction. The greed and success motivations are two of the most powerful tools used by Satan against a writer. So don't begin to write because you seek fame and fortune; it is a satanic notion. Write because God ordained it, and the Holy Spirit supports it.

I must digress here for a moment and talk about how secular success stories in the arts take place in Satan's world because the process exacts an extreme price. It has been noted that if you want to be successful as an artist that you must live where the wheels of success are located. I have heard that an artist can only become nationally known if they live in New York City and Los Angeles. These two metropolitan areas confer to the remainder of the United States who is an artist and for what reason. Therefore, to become a nationally famous artist, you must move to a location where success can find you. Chicago is often used as a third location where a successful artist can promote a national career by establishing a Midwest following. But most nationally known artists use New York or LA as a springboard to success because the levers of power are also located there. According to the New York or LA residence formula, if you live in a small town in rural America, you don't stand a chance of being recognized at the national level. Publishing houses in both cities receive thousands of book manuscripts every year that they throw into what's known as a slush pile, where they will probably never be read. Without a New York or LA literary agent and without a track record living in those cities, the odds that a manuscript will get published diminishes. It's true that some unknown mid-American writers have surfaced out of this chaos by Divine Providence. But most famous authors become famous because they knew how to play the game of getting noticed from millions of other writers. And this requires being near the action where agents and publishers reside.

To make matters worse for those unknown writers who live in rural US areas, there is a multitude of unscrupulous operators between them and national success who promote for a price that same fame and fortune illusion. I get telephone calls every day from people who want to promote my writing for a price; the calls register as Potential Spam on my cell phone. Most of the time, I am too busy writing to answer them, but when I do answer them, I usually ask only one question: name one book or movie that I know that you have promoted successfully to a national audience. Usually, they hang up the phone or change the subject. In short, Satan will provide the illusion of becoming a successful author to an unknown writer for a price tag. Last week, I received a form letter from one of these questionable entities who wanted to promote one of my books into a movie. Unfortunately, they didn't bother to read the book because it couldn't possibly be made into a movie. So, writers not only have to contend with the arduous tasks of writing and creating good books, but they also have to contend with the secular intrusions of Satan as misguided interference to get them published. And, even if an artist moves to New York or LA, they still must make the right connections to succeed, and these connections mean being in the right place at the right time to meet the right people.

For a songwriter In Nashville, this means buying drinks at night in bars for the right record label producers and promoters, which means spending a lot of money to become buddy/buddy with successful and influential people in the music business. Of course, these influential people already know that you've an unknown songwriter and that you must make them happy, so they accept the drinks that you buy them night after night and endure your conversations until the shoe drops with the sales pitch for your song, whereupon they find other unknown songwriters who can buy them more drinks. From my experience, songwriters who move to Nashville to follow this formula don't live long, even though they might get a few songs published for their efforts. I know that all this discussion sounds negative, and it should. It is hell-bound in its origins.

Questions
1. Who leads people to their vocations?
2. How does the complication of being an over-consumer influence a writer?
3. Why doesn't Satan want moderation?
4. Who is the author of your life?

CHAPTER 4 SOME LITERARY WORKS INFLUENCED BY THE HOLY SPIRIT

Essay 24 JOHN CHEEVER: The Enormous Radio

Writers want to understand themselves and the world better by providing a thematic window that reduces the world's chaos for the reader to one thematic point. In fact, many writers have been successful at capturing the cultural and social moment of the time. For instance, John Cheever's short story "The Enormous Radio" depicts the essence of the post WWII US culture by providing the thematic elements close to the spiritual heart of the American Dream. In the "Enormous Radio," Cheever sets the scene in a Manhattan apartment in 1947 while Levittown was being built from 1947 to 1951. Levittown was the forerunner to suburban sub-divisions where uniformity of construction was utilized to make housing affordable. Rows of the same houses were occupied by two parents with two children, preferably a boy and a girl, and one dog. All the rows of identical houses had perfectly manicured lawns and a shiny new car on a concrete driveway. In this setting, from the outside of the house, the inside of the house's world would appear just as idyllic. However, it wasn't, nor was the apartment occupied by Jim and Irene Westcott. When Jim and Irene Westcott buy a new console radio for their Manhattan apartment in pre-television days, instead of receiving news and music broadcasted by the radio stations they receive the conversations of their neighbors in the apartments surrounding them. Jim and Irene Westcott were social climbers; they attended the theater 10.3 times per year and have dreams of owning their own home someday, probably in Levittown. Yet, the private conversations inside the apartments surrounding them didn't reflect the idyllic nature of the American Dream and cast doubt on their future. The conversations between young couples in other apartments ranged from arguments about spending too much money to infidelity accusations. In short, the ideal façade of Jim and Irene Westcott owning their own home someday and living happily ever after is shattered by the voices of their fellow apartment dwellers. When the lives of their fellow apartment dwellers were viewed from the outside, their lives appeared to be fine. However, when viewed from inside, the idyllic American dream is compromised by the frailties of human nature. This fragile view of the American Dream wasn't limited to only their apartment building, but it existed all over America and was embodied in the new rising middle class.

While the retooled factories of the post WWII United States economy were churring out refrigerators and stoves instead of bombs for the rising middle class who would dwell in housing developments like Levittown, Cheever realized that the concept of the American Dream was based on the false premise that putting your trust in people, upward social mobility, and possessions was an error. In short, the possessions of newly found middle class wealth couldn't buy happiness. The Bible also makes this point. Under Satan's temporary control of the earth, happiness cannot be derived from acquiring material things. True happiness stems from a spiritual relationship with God through Jesus and the Holy Spirit. "Set your affection on things above, not on things on the earth" (Colossians 3:2) In addition, Cheever's theme in the "Enormous Radio" also echoes the Bible verse, "Lay not up for yourselves treasures upon the earth, where moth and rust doeth corrupt, and where thieves break through and steal: For where your treasure is, there will your heart be also" (Matthew 6:20-21). Whether Cheever intended to echo Bible verse or not, who knows? But one thing is for sure, he did it, whether consciously or unconsciously. And by doing so, he injected America with a basic biblical truth in an otherwise misguided world.

In addition, in the short story "The Enormous Radio" John Cheever uses a supernatural force to take over the radio's broadcasting to produce the conversations of people in neighboring apartments. No physical explanation for the supernatural event will suffice; for whatever the reason the couple's new console radio has tapped into the private conversations of their neighbors. Understanding how this phenomenon works is impossible; it is something that goes beyond human comprehension and flows in a stream of supernatural energy. In short, understanding how their radio works is impossible. It's like someone trying to tell someone else how the Holy Spirit communicates with them. In "The Enormous Radio," the element of supernatural communication through the radio creates a moral problem. When Jim and Irene Westcott first discover that their radio is broadcasting the private conversations of their neighbors, they had to ask themselves a moral question: Should they be listening to other people's private conversations? By asking this moral question about whether they should listen, Cheever has allowed the Holy Spirit to intervene, and now it is up to the Westcott's free will to choose between being good or doing evil. The Holy Spirit has conveyed to them through their Spirit's conscience that to listen to the private conversation of their neighbors on the radio is sinful. Yet, they chose to listen anyway and to follow Satan instead of following God and the Holy Spirit's advice.

Thus, the Westcott's free will choice about whether to follow the Holy Spirit's advice or Satan's advice is apparent in Cheever's story. The Holy Spirit probably inspired Cheever to give his fictional characters a moral choice of whether to do good or evil. Cheever didn't have to include this moral choice in his story; it could have been totally a secular story about the existence or nonexistence of the American Dream. But it wasn't. To me, the Holy Spirit through the author placed the moral dilemma to listen or not to the private conversations of neighbors to emphasize the spiritual quality found in the story. The fact that nobody living in the neighborhood is living like the pristine exterior of their outward appearances is the social theme, yet the larger moral theme that Cheever implied was whether we should listen to something in the media just because it is broadcast to us on bandwidth? Looking at how the salacious content of "The Enormous Radio" gripped the minds of the Westcott's reminds me of how the internet has exponentially advanced Cheever's moral theme years later? In short, whether to watch or listen to internet content is still a free will moral choice. Therefore, at the very beginnings of mass media Cheever had anticipated a moral problem related to it. Thus, through the Holy Spirit writers are inspired to write about moral conduct (Cheever). "…the Spirit itself maketh intercession for us…And he that searcheth the hearts knoweth what is the mind of the Spirit" (Romans 8:26-27)].

Essay 25 KURT VONNEGUT Breakfast of Champions

The novelist Kurt Vonnegut, a professed atheist, also provided a biblical truth about the existence of the spiritual self in his novel *Breakfast of Champions.* In the novel, Vonnegut enters his own novel as a character. While "self-insertion" is a literary device in which the author writes himself or herself into the story as a fictional character, it is not recommended because it crosses the author - fictional character line of believability. *In the Breakfast of Champions*, Vonnegut's fictional version of himself is first seen standing in a restaurant kitchen. At this time, the author pauses the plot of his novel to debate with himself about whether he should enter is own novel as a character. The author's internal debate reveals some spiritual insight. First, by dividing himself into both author and fictional character, Vonnegut becomes two people -- not one. Later, in an interview, he called the entering his own novel as a character "the spiritual climax of the book." Therefore, by dividing himself into two separate people, Vonnegut ultimately realizes that a second person exists within him. For him, the second person might be only himself as a fictional character, but it indicates the possibility of a second being existing within him, much like a Christian recognizes him or herself as two people -- the physical and spiritual self. He further continues this spirituality theme when he states, "at the core of each person who reads this book is a band of unwavering light." For everyone, this band of unwavering light is God, and God never changes; God is unwavering. Therefore, at this moment in his novel Vonnegut recognizes something spiritual about himself and says that there is, "something sacred at his core" (231). Furthermore, at the end of his novel Vonnegut sets all his characters free from the novel. He liberates them from their physical selves on the page, just like Christians when accepting Jesus as Lord and Savior become liberated them from their physical selves on earth. To Vonnegut -- like with every author -- his characters are not just fictional characters but living extensions of himself. In fact, he sets one character, Kilgore Trout, free from the novel because he is living in the novel "under similar spiritual conditions." Therefore, when writing *Breakfast of Champions* Vonnegut found some spiritual dimension of himself by becoming an extension of himself as a fictional character. In short, Vonnegut was being <u>guided</u> by the Holy Spirit while writing *Breakfast of Champions* to a moment of spiritual realization. I believe that it was a special moment in Vonnegut's writing life when the hand of God reached out for the hand of an avowed atheist to provide spiritual awareness (Vonnegut, *Breakfast*).

    Therefore, many writers through their thematic pursuits have always been on a quest to better understand human nature. By doing so, much of their work reflects a spiritual pursuit as the Holy Spirit reveals to them the deep things of God. Whether the authors intended to project an underlying deeper spiritual message, no one will ever know for sure. Writers are also notorious for being evasive about commenting on their own work. I believe that's because they, themselves, don't totally understand their writing because of the Holy Spirit's influence. Yet sometimes the spiritual connection between how an author constructs their writing and its biblical parallel cannot be ignored. For example, in Vonnegut's *Breakfast of Champions* the swinging kitchen door in the restaurant has a glass window where Vonnegut can peer into the dining room, where his characters are talking. At this point, when Vonnegut pauses to decide whether to enter his own novel, this glass window indicates that he can see through to the other side just like Believers in Jesus Christ can see through to their spiritual side. The Bible states that we, too, can step away from our physical lives and into our spiritual lives by walking through a door." ... behold, I set before thee an open door, and no man can shut it: for thou hast little strength, and kept my word, and has not denied my name" (Revelation 3:8). Therefore, God is a Spirit, and the Spirit is giving us an invitation to walk through the door and into our own spiritual lives. To further illustrate this point: "Behold, I stand at the door, and knock: if any man hear my voice and open the door, I will come into him, and will sup with him, and he with me." (Revelation 3:20). While stopping before walking through the swinging kitchen door in the restaurant to become a character in his own novel door and thinking about what to do, it is as if Vonnegut is asking the Holy Spirit for help. At this moment, Vonnegut is really taking a leap of faith. If he uses the unorthodox literary device of entering his own novel as a character, he needs the assurance of the Holy Spirit that it will work. Ultimately, Vonnegut –as a character – pushes open the kitchen door and walks into the restaurant's dining room to dialogue with his other fictional characters.

I'm sure that when Kurt Vonnegut started writing *Breakfast of Champions,* he didn't have himself entering his own novel as a character. In fact, he probably wouldn't have even considered it; that is, until the Holy Spirit inspired him.

Questions
1. How does *The Enormous Radio* by John Cheever exhibit the influence of the Holy Spirit?
2. How does the moral theme in *The Enormous Radio* coincide with today's internet?
3. Do you think Vonnegut relied on the Holy Spirit's advice before entering his own novel?
4. Do you think Vonnegut had a spiritual awakening by writing *Breakfast of Champions*?

Essay 26 JOSEPH HELLER: Catch 22

In Joseph Heller's novel *Catch 22*, there is a character named Major, Major. The character's last name is Major, and the first Major in his name is his military rank. Major, Major's office hours are indicative of the logic found in the military. Because Major, Major doesn't want anyone to visit him in his office, he instructs his doorkeeper underlings to tell people who want to see him: That he is only "in" when he is "out" and that he is "out" when he is "in." In this way, Major, Major avoids any dialogue that might cause him trouble. The entire *Catch 22* novel by Joseph Heller comments on the comic absurdities of war. As the dark, comedic absurdities continue, the reader both laughs and cries. Essentially, the novel is really an anti-war novel. Heller was a WWII veteran and saw the absurdities of war first-hand. He knew first-hand how little war accomplished and how large its cost. By the end of the novel, the reader just shakes their head about the illogical logic that Heller presents.

Many of Heller's characters in *Catch 22* represent many of the flaws found in human nature, which become reoccurring moral themes. The greed of Milo Minderbinder, the anxiety and fear of Doc Daneeka, and the dead man in Yossarian's tent. There is a dead man in Yossarian's tent that everyone ignores because they don't want to believe that he is dead. Likewise, many people in life ignore the physically dead person living within themselves. From the moment that we are born, the process of dying begins. Some people don't like to address the "death issue" and choose to avoid coming to terms with it and talking about it, just like the characters in Catch 22 chose to ignore the dead man in Yossarian's tent by not talking about him. Ignoring death is a spiritual matter. Because the characters in the novel cannot face the truth, they have also abandoned the spiritual side of themselves. However, anyone – including writers –who live in their Spirit and is saved by Jesus is not afraid of death because they will be going to live with Him in heaven. Therefore, for a saved Christian physical death gives rise to a new spiritual life. So, at the heart of the gift of salvation given by Jesus Christ is the gift of eternal life with Him. For a Christian, earth is just a horrible way station on their way to living and finally finding peace with Jesus in heaven. Therefore, in *Catch 22* by ignoring the dead body in Yossarian's tent that no one wanted to acknowledge, Joseph Heller is making a spiritual point about recognizing and dealing with your own physical demise, and this reoccurring point in the novel is a Spirit-inspired one.

Joseph Heller in *Catch 22* also address the issue of having faith. Yossarian, a bombardier, wants out of the war because he sees its deadly absurdities, much like aware Christians see Satan's absurdities on earth. In the novel, every time that Yossarian nears the cap on the number of combat-flying missions, the military brass raises the cap. Therefore, what might have started out as a 20-combat mission tour to return home, now has increased to 30,40, and 50 combat missions. With his hope of going home dwindling by the ever-increasing number of combat missions, Yossarian begins to understand that he might never make it home. This ever-increasing escalation of bombing missions also represents the unknown number of days in our own lives and tribulations. Who hasn't counted on something big happening in their own life, only to have their hopes dashed when it didn't happen? Thus, Heller's war novel is also about our own conflict with life.

A writer knows many of the bitter disappointments in life: rejection slip after rejection slip from publishers, bad reviews, the dead zone of no promotion, never finding a readership, and people asking when you're getting a real job. Thus, a writers' life is filled with the unknowns of disappointment where expectations don't meet reality, and they should heed the spiritual <u>comfort</u> and <u>encouragement</u> supplied by Holy Spirit and read the Bible. Jesus' words in the Bible inspire hope in a world fraught with Satan's disappointments.

Therefore, one of *Catch 22*'s themes is that living solely in the secular world will not inspire hope and that these secular disappointments –like the increase in the number of bombing missions -- will outlast even the strongest of determined human will. By contrast, it takes a spiritual connection with Jesus through the Holy Spirit to inspire faith which, in turn, inspires hope. For a writer turning to Jesus through the Holy Spirit to find <u>hope</u> is essential because Satan's aim is to instill hopelessness in all of us. Many times, I've seen this hopelessness on the faces of potentially good writers. Yet, at least for now their eyes simply don't reflect the strength of the Spirit within them. Ironically, their eyes have the secular determination of succeeding in the world, but their eyes do not reflect the serenity of hope in the future as found in the Holy Spirit. In *Catch 22* Yossarian reaches this hopeless point in his life because the military brass keeps increasing the number of combat missions. "The enemy is anybody who's going to get you killed, no matter which side he's on …." (124). This reflects Yossarian's reliance on the secular world for answers. Like war, the secular world is often brutal because Satan likes it that way because at times all things instill a sense of hopelessness. However, God doesn't want it that way. God – through Jesus and the Holy Spirit – wants love and peace.

Thus, *Catch 22* is a dark novel that exposes the absurdities of war where the characters also represent people at war with themselves. Yet, while Heller raises numerous spiritual questions about life and death in *Catch 22*, the important point is that most people accept the absurdities of war and life as normal. The characters' actions are much like real life where people unthinkingly go through life and feel doomed by the weight of Satan's world upon them but don't pray for Spiritual help from Jesus for relief. War is probably the ultimate secular experience, and the military doesn't want a spiritual perspective because it might diminish the morale of the troops. The military doesn't want a soldier to think about

God and about what to do. The military just wants blind obedience to follow orders. This is one reason why Heller's novel is important because his depiction of war's absurdities as the only answer issues forth the question: Isn't there a better way? And that better way is through the Holy Spirit and the peace found in the saving grace of Jesus (Heller).

Questions
1. Who gives a writer the insight into their own time period's society and culture?
2. Name some of the connections between war and human nature in *Catch 22*.
3. Has the number of bombing missions ever been raised in your life?
4. How does a writer's expectations for their work coincide with the bombing missions?

Essay 27 T.S. ELIOT: The Love Song of J Alfred Prufrock

In *the Love Song of J Alfred Prufrock*, a poem by T.S. Elliot, the character in the poem is going older and he starts to second guess himself about life. He states, "Time for you and time for me. And time yet for a hundred indecisions, and for a hundred visions and revisions." Thus, Elliot addresses how difficult it is to really know your place in life by rationally editing through it. To him, nothing seems to be finished or truthful about living. One of Elliot's most famous verses is found in the same poem; it's a verse that talks about the phoniness of playing roles in life. "There will be time, there will be time. To prepare a face to meet the faces that you meet." In other words, we all play roles for other people in our lives, and while playing those numerous roles in life we often diminish the essence of ourselves. I believe that these types of larger spiritual wisdoms about life are prompted by the Holy Spirit. If we fraudulently play too many roles during our lifetime, we can forget about who we really are and lose our own identity.

While the characters in a novel or poem have no choice but to follow the writer's directions, in life people do have a choice by free will about whether to follow God to choose their soul's destination. Being a god-author in the world of book illusion is nothing like being the real and only God and Author of the Universe. At times, writers feel like they are writing alone in the darkness of their own despair. However, in real life, people (writers) do have the free will to pray for the Holy Spirit to offer hope and to make choices to elicit changes in themselves. Writers in real life do have a choice. They can follow the evil perpetuated by Satan and incorporate his sin into their life, or they can follow God, Jesus Christ, and the Holy Spirit by making choices that are good for them and good for their writing.

Unlike fiction characters who blindly follow the direction of the author, God has given people the free will to choose how they want to live their life. The choices between doing good or evil might seem numerous over a lifetime, and they are. However, the many choices presented to you in the world over a lifetime only come down to one overriding choice: whether to live your life in Satan's darkness or in God's light. You can put your faith in Jesus and the Holy Spirit for writing direction, or you can choose the evil ways of the devil. T.S Elliot in his poem *The Love Song of J Alfred Prufrock* also addresses the question of mortality and the choices one makes in life. Again, it is the Holy Spirit's <u>guidance</u> that provides the <u>direction</u> towards these types of <u>inspirational</u> and spiritual moments. "I have seen the moment of my greatness flicker, and I have seen the eternal Footman, hold my coat, and snicker. And in short, I was afraid." Granted, it's only a fictional character in one of Elliot's poems who admits that he is afraid of death because the Eternal footman is holding his coat, thus saying that he is nearing the time to go to his eternal destination, either heaven or hell. Yet, by addressing the question of mortality, Elliot is really asking the reader to rise above the chaos of Satan's temporary control of the world to connect with God's comforting Spirit to avoid life's confusion, and this connection is made through Jesus sending His Holy Spirit to us. So, not being afraid of death is a Christian concept that results from having a spiritual connection with God through Jesus who gave us the Holy Spirit to comfort us. "For God is not the author of confusion but of peace" (1 Corinthians 14:33). By making good choices in life with God's guidance through Jesus and the Holy Spirit, writers become closer to God (<u>sanctification</u>) and His blessing for their own writing. T.S. Elliot knew that our single choice in life was whether to do good or evil; clearly he is being influenced by the Holy Spirit when in the latter part of his poem J. Alfred Prufrock states, "When the wind blows the water white and black." That is, when the wind of life gives us choices of white (good) and black (evil) (Eliot).

Essay 28 Conclusion: Connotation, Denotation, and the Holy Spirit

If you look up a word in the dictionary, it will give you the literal meaning. For instance, if you look up the word *bathroom* in the dictionary, other words that literally mean the same thing will be listed. Logically, you might encounter in the dictionary the following words as meaning the same as *bathroom* -- *restroom, toilet, lavatory, washroom,* and *powder room*. According to the dictionary's denotative and literal meaning, all these words mean the same thing. However, from these corresponding words for *bathroom* found in the dictionary, I can also use the implied connotative meaning to indicate each word's location and cleanliness; therefore, an implied or connotative meaning can further extend the literal meaning of the word. For instance, which is connotatively more hygienic a toilet or a restroom? A restroom is, of course. Where would you find them? A toilet would be found in a greasy gas station, and a restroom would be found in a restaurant. If you are a woman at the opera, and at intermission you ask an usher where the toilet is located, they will probably give you directions to the powder room. The opera doesn't have a toilet. Lavatories are found on airplanes; heads are found on ships; latrines are found in an army barracks, and bathrooms are found in houses. Therefore, a denotative meaning of a word is one-dimensional; it states that all words are alike and found in the same place and have the same level of cleanliness, whereas the connotative or implied meaning indicates certain attributes of the word that extends the meaning and distinguishes it from other words. It is the connotative meaning that involves the Holy Spirit because it requires creatively using your imagination to see the difference between words in your mind's eye. For example, when I wrote the word *toilet* as an alternate word for *bathroom*, I cringed when I instantly remembered the horrible condition of a greasy 1950's gas station toilet in the middle of the desert in Nevada. Accordingly, being able to decipher a lifetime of experience into certain limited moments is the Holy Spirit's gift of <u>remembrance</u> to a writer. These moments are remembered for the moral lessons that they taught. Some memories are good, and some are bad, but they all have lasted a lifetime because of the Holy Spirit's promptings, which relay to the writer the moral significance of the event. Thus, connotative meanings rely heavily on mind pictures of the events that allude to the moral lesson learned. Whereas the denotative meaning only requires the phonetic sounding out of the word and knowing its literal meaning, the connotative version of a word requires an active imagination to reconstruct the memory to make the association between word, place, and cleanliness.

It is much like the difference between watching television and listening to the same story on the radio. Watching a story on the television is one-dimensional because it provides everything. If a car in the story screeches to a halt, the television visually provides the model of car, the color of the car, and the year of the car. Therefore, no imaginative thought is required of the viewer. However, if the same story is listened to on a radio, then the listener's active imagination and participation are required. For every listener of the story on a radio, the car is a different model, color, and year in their own mind. Some listeners imagine that the car is blue, some green, and some red. Some imagine it as a Chevy, others a Ford, and some a Honda. Therefore, television viewing is a passive form of entertainment because it requires little imagination and thought from the viewer. Everything is visually supplied. On the other hand, radio is an active form of entertainment because the listener is constantly using their imagination to fill in the blanks. This contrast between television being a passive form of entertainment and radio being an active form of entertainment is much like the difference between denotation being one dimensional and connotation being multi-dimensional. In turn, it is also like living your life without Jesus and the Holy Spirit in the one-dimensional realm of only the physical world. While the physical world of Satan pretends to supply everything you need in life, it leaves out the most important element –namely, the spiritual individuality of you. Satan's world is one dimensional much like watching tv. Satan provides everything that you think you need, including possessions, power, and money. But the one-dimensional world of Satan does not include peace of mind through knowing your own spiritual self through Jesus and the Holy Spirit. The knowledge of your own holiness extends your one-dimensional physical life by including your spiritual life and Jesus' gift of salvation that becomes life after death in heaven. Satan's here and now perspective might seem like a huge party for the moment, but eventually everyone goes home after the party is over and all that is left is the mess associated with the occasion. It is a fact that life is messy, and Satan will provide your part in this mess if you let him because he makes it so chaotic that no one can figure out life without the saving grace of Jesus and the guidance of the Holy Spirit. Keep this in mind the next time you sit down to write. Without these spiritual acknowledgements, life is just a one-dimensional physical life-and-death arrangement with Satan controlling you and eventually steering your soul to hell. For the moment, Satan's television world of supplying everything physically for you without you having to think about the destination of your soul might be entertaining, but as years accumulate your life and everything in it will eventually grow boring from being supplied with everything that Satan thinks you need. Overall, what Satan can't supply is permanent happiness and hope. The real difference between knowing Jesus in life and living beyond your physical self in your spiritual self and not knowing

Him as your personal savior is found in the amount of joy found in life by the inclusion of spiritual participation. Just like the connotative meaning adds emotional content and extends the meaning of a word because the reader acknowledges the variables beyond a one-dimensional denotative meaning, the Holy Spirit does much the same thing by stimulating the writers' active imagination to include the awareness of the spiritual self. By doing so, both the writer's life and their writing's content create extended versions of the meaning of life that are not otherwise available. Therefore, Jesus through the Holy Spirit makes a writer aware of these spiritual possibilities to expand their physical life both in the moral meaning found in their life and in their writing. Multiple complexities exist in life, and to view life as only a one-dimensional physical version through Satan's eyes is a huge mistake. Without the power and blessing of God through Jesus and the Holy Spirit being with you in life, your existence will remain one-dimensional and grounded to earth, whereas a life lived for God in the Spirit with Jesus Christ extends to you all the power of heavenly possibilities.

REFERENCES

Gardner, Howard. *The Compositions of Mozart's Mind. Art, Mind, and Brain*. Harper, 1982.

Philo of Alexandria. *DeVita Moysis,* 111, no. 23.

Metzger and Coogen, MD. The Oxford Companion to the Bible. Oxford University Press. 1993, p302-304.

Swayer, MJ. "Theories of Inspiration." http/wwwbible.org/.

Lea, Thomas Dale; Griffin, Jr., Hayne Preston. *The New American Commentary* (1,2 Timothy, Titus), vol. 34, Nashville, TN: Broadman and Homan Publishers, 1992.

Woolf, Virginia. "Boxing Day." *A Writer's Diary*. Nota Bene Books, 1953.

Niemetsckek, Franz. *Mozart: The First Biography*. Berghan Books, 2006.

Thurber, James. "The Greatest Man in the World," *New Yorker Magazine*, Feb 13, 1931, p 20.

Warren, Robert Penn. *New and Selected Poems 1923-1985*. Random House, 1985.

Random House Webster's College Dictionary. Random House Inc., 2000, p 1500.

Gardner, Howard. *The Compositions of Mozart's Mind. Art, Mind, and Brain*. Harper, 1982.

Davis, Merilyn L. "Swoopers and Bashers and Words! Oh My!" *To Drops of Ink.com* December27, 2019.

Edel, Leon. *Henry James Letters*, 1895- 1916, Vol. 4, 1925, p.105.

James, Henry. *The American.* James R. Osgood & Co., May 5, 1877.

Vonnegut, Kurt. "Harrison Bergeron" *Welcome to the Monkey House*. Delacorte Press,1968.

Thoreau, Henry David. *Walden Pond; Life in the Woods*. Boston. Ticknor & Fields, 1854.

Random House Webster's College Dictionary. Random House. New York, 2000, p 377.

Bradbury, Ray. *Fahrenheit 451*. Ballantine Books, Oct 19, 1953.

Vonnegut, Kurt. *Player Piano*. Chares Scribner's & Sons, Aug 18, 1952.

Salinger, JD. *Catcher in the Rye*. Little Brown. New York, July 16, 1951.

Wisnewski, Jesse. "24 Must Know Characteristics of the Holy Spirit" https//get.tithe.ly/blog, July 8,2020.

Moody Bible Institute. "The Person and Word of the Holy Spirit," moodybible.org.

Cheever, John. "The Enormous Radio," *The New Yorker Magazine*, May 17, 1947.

Vonnegut, Kurt. *Breakfast of Champions*. Dial Press, May 11, 1999.

Heller, Joseph. *Catch 22*. Simon & Schuster. New York, November 10, 1961.

Eliot, TS. "The Love Song of J. Alfred Prufrock." *Poetry Magazine of Verse*, June 1915.

Other titles from Higher Ground Books & Media:

Chronicles of a Spiritual Journey by Stephen Shepherd

Eyes of Understanding by Stephen Shepherd

Losing the Sound of Your Own Stride by Stephen Shepherd

The Power of Knowing by Jean Walters

Forgiven and Not Forgotten by Terra Kern

Oasis or Mirage by Terra Kern

The Deception of 666 by Terra Kern

Bits & Pieces by Rebecca Whited

Raven Transcending Fear by Terri Kozlowski

Through the Sliver of a Frosted Window by Robin Melet

Breaking the Cycle by Willie Deeanjlo White

Man Made by Grace by Willie Deeanjlo White

For His Eyes Only by John Salmon, Ph. D

A Practical Guide to Better Behaved Children by John Salmon, Ph. D

The Real Prison Diaries by Judy Frisby

The Words of My Father by Mark Nemetz

The Bottom of This by Tramaine Hannah

Add these titles to your collection today!

http://www.highergroundbooksandmedia.com

HIGHER GROUND BOOKS & MEDIA IS AN INDEPENDENT PUBLISHER

Do you have a story to tell?

Higher Ground Books & Media is an independent Christian-based publisher specializing in stories of triumph! Our purpose is to empower, inspire, and educate through the sharing of personal experiences. We are always looking for great, new stories to add to our collection. If you're looking for a publisher, get in touch with us today!

Please be sure to visit our website for our submission guidelines.

http://www.highergroundbooksandmedia.com/submission-guidelines

HGBM SERVICES IS OUR CONSULTING FIRM

AUTHOR SERVICES

HGBM Services offers a variety of writing and coaching services for aspiring authors! We can help with editing, manuscript critiques, self-publishing, and much more! Get in touch today to see how we can help you make your dream of becoming an author a reality!

*****

We also offer social media marketing services for authors, small businesses, and non-profit organizations. Let us help you get the word out about your book, your projects, and your mission. We offer great rates, quality promos, consistent communication, and a personal touch!

http://www.highergroundbooksandmedia.com/editing-writing-services

Need Bulk Copies?

If you would like to order bulk copies of this book or any other title at Higher Ground Books & Media, please contact us at highergroundbooksandmedia@gmail.com.

We offer discounts for purchases of 20 or more copies. Excellent for small groups, book clubs, classrooms, etc.

Get in touch today and get a set of great stories for your students or group members.

www.ingramcontent.com/pod-product-compliance
Lightning Source LLC
Chambersburg PA
CBHW061439040426
42450CB00007B/1123